9 Ways
to Bring Out
the Best in
You & Your Child

Maggie Reigh

9 Ways
TO Bring Out
THE Best IN
You & Your
Child

Northstone

Editor: Michael Schwartzentruber
Cover and interior design: Margaret Kyle
Proofreading: Dianne Greenslade
Front cover photo: © Kristy-Anne Glubish, www.designpics.com. Used by permission.
Back cover photo: © www.photos.com. Used by permission. Author photo: Margaret Kyle
Interior illustrations: © Arleigh Dudar (Maggie's daughter). Used by permission.
Calligraphy on page 28: © Peizhong Chen. Used by permission.
Emotions chart on page 235: © Megan Matz. Used by permission.

Northstone Publishing is an imprint of Wood Lake Books, Inc. Wood Lake Books acknowledges the
financial support of the Government of Canada, through the Book Publishing Industry Development
Program (BPIDP) for its publishing activities.

Wood Lake Books is an employee-owned company, committed to caring for the environment
and all creation. Wood Lake Books recycles, reuses, and encourages readers to do the same.
Resources are printed on recycled paper and more environmentally friendly groundwood papers
(newsprint), whenever possible. The trees used are replaced through donations to the Scoutrees
For Canada Program. A percentage of all profit is donated to charitable organizations.

Library and Archives Canada Cataloguing in Publication
Reigh, Maggie, 1955–
9 ways to bring out the best in you & your child / Maggie Reigh.
Includes index.
ISBN 1-896836-64-X
1. Parenting. 2. Child rearing. I. Title. II. Title: Nine ways to bring
out the best in you and your child.
HQ769.R42 2004   649'.1   C2004-903909-1

Published by Northstone Publishing
an imprint of WOOD LAKE BOOKS, INC.
9025 Jim Bailey Road, Kelowna, BC, Canada, V4V 1R2
250.766.2778
www.northstone.com

Printing 10 9 8 7 6 5 4 3 2 1
Printed in Canada by Transcontinental

Dedication

I dedicate this book to my three wonderful and spirited children:
Jason, Tyler, and Arleigh
– my greatest teachers of love, joy, inner strength,
and personal power.
And to my parents,
for their immense love and support,
and for their unwavering belief in me.

Table of Contents

Notes from Maggie's children

You are my mother and my friend,
Which is unusual.
Somehow our characters must still blend:
Your wisdom and my will.

I turn, and you are there for me;
I speak, you understand;
I feel cared for, but also free;
You lead, but don't command.

I'm fortunate that I was born
To someone just like you,
I love you, not just as my mom,
But for what you are and do.

ARLEIGH

Mom,
Thank you for teaching me to look at the bright side. Thank you for having patience and letting me tell you my troubles. You have shown me that being happy and getting to know yourself are a big part of life, you live it everyday and are an inspiration to me.

JASON

Mom,
Over the years you have encouraged us to do the things we love to do. Your encouragement has empowered our knowledge, creativity, physical awareness, and love for all beings. For this I love you...

TYLER

Acknowledgements

I would like to express my deep gratitude and appreciation to the people who have supported and encouraged me in the birthing of this book:

- To my children who allowed me to share our stories, and who supported me in the practicalities of taking care of our home while encouraging me to follow my passion.
- To my 13-year-old daughter, Arleigh, for providing the artwork.
- To my mom, whose spirit of unconditional love forms the backbone of this book, and to my dad, who ignited within me the search for truth and peace.
- To all of my friends, family, and colleagues who provided encouragement and support in so many ways. Special thanks to
  - ~ Yvonne Novakowski, for her intellectual guidance and heartfelt input throughout the writing of this book;
  - ~ Beverly Hunter, for her listening ear, her passion for this work, and her unwavering dedication in championing the rights of children;
  - ~ Lynn Malinsky, for her vision, inspiration and leadership in parenting education and community development;
  - ~ Robert Kirkman, for his love and support, and for his enthusiastic promotion of this work;
  - ~ the first facilitators of this course, for their patience, honest feedback, enthusiasm, and encouragement: Myrna Kalmakoff, Gail Wolanski, Tracy Roshinsky, Kyla Ashman,

Teresa Bouchard, Oneala Bell, Donna Bergvinson, Angela Rock, Barb Zeitner, Deborah Swan, Christy Phillips, Rick Jones, Yvonne McIsaac, Angel Fehr, and Masami Kostiuk.

~ Elizabeth Van Dyk, my *Parenting with Purpose* co-facilitator, for her encouragement, support, and practical expertise in arranging seminars and meeting parents' needs.

- To the team at Wood Lake Books for their warm and enthusiastic reception and promotion of this book – to Lois Huey-Heck for her initial encouragement and steadfast support in seeing this project through from the beginning; to Margaret Kyle for her enthusiastic support and expertise in artistic design; and to my publicist, Cassandra Redding. Special thanks to Mike Schwartzentruber, whose wisdom and professional expertise in editing proved that "an editor is my friend"!
- To the many parents from courses and consultations over the years, who've shared their wisdom and experiences.
- To Okanagan Families Society, who provided the structure and support to offer programs to parents.
- To the wisdom gleaned from numerous parenting educators.

Resources

- For information on Maggie's presentations and seminars for parents, educators, and businesses, visit her website at www.maggiereigh.com or call toll free 1-866-263-7741. Maggie has CDs and stories for people of all ages.
- For a practical and delightful approach to learning how to take charge of your inner environment and to helping your children take charge of theirs, refer to the *Who's Driving this Bus Anyway* CD by Maggie Reigh.
- For information on Educational Kinesiology and Brain Gym check out www.turningonthelight.com.

Introduction

My daughter, Arleigh, was almost a year old when she convinced me that taking some parenting classes might be a good idea! That's when I found out that I was truly not alone in my parental struggles and concerns and pride and joy.

With a background in education and childcare, I really thought that this parenting job should be easy. After all, before having children of my own, I had *all* the answers to my siblings' and friends' parental woes. I'm sure everyone was relieved when I finally began my own family.

I then realized that parenting is a lot harder on the inside than it looks from the outside. I remember looking down at my white-knuckled hand as it held shut the door to my young son's room. My three-year-old hurled his body against it on the other side, screaming, "Let me out of here! You can't keep me in here! It's not fair!"

"*This*," I thought, "is time out? There *has* to be a more effective way to discipline! This is not what I had in mind. I mean, if I tell him his behavior is inappropriate and send him off to his room, shouldn't he just go?"

That incident started my search for more effective – and peaceful – ways to raise my children, and though I had challenges with the boys, reading some parenting books helped a lot.

Then along came Arleigh! Arleigh came into this world screaming at the top of her lungs. Fiery red hair, intense blue eyes, and a voracious appetite were early indications of the very precious gift, and challenge, that awaited me. Emotionally sensitive and very expressive, Arleigh lived in a world of extremes. When she wasn't completely delighting us, she was often enraged – and she spent a *great deal* of her early years in a tearful rage. Her frustration and anguish were intensified by her eczema, a skin condition creating extreme itching and irritation.

Arleigh's rage could be set off by a sideways glance containing the smallest *hint* of frustration on my part. I remember shopping with her when she was three. She was happily pushing her own "Little Shopper's Cart" when she ran into my heel.

"Ouch!" I cried. "Arleigh, be careful!" I gasped, as I reached down to rub my heel.

This was enough to set Arleigh off completely. She broke into a piercing wail, "A-h-h-h-h-h-h! I HATE YOU-OU-OU-OU!!!!" and ran off, screaming, at high speed down the nearest grocery isle, pushing her little cart in front of her, careening around corners, and narrowly missing the shoppers who leaped out of the way.

My first reaction was shock. By the time I realized what had happened, she was already well out of my reach, so I just let her go and focused on staying calm – and, I hoped, inconspicuous as well. I wanted to hide. I knew from experience that even when I caught her there would be no way to *make* her stop screaming. I could just imagine the comments from the other shoppers: "Yes, and did you know her mother *teaches* parenting classes?"

Trying to ignore both Arleigh's screaming and the voices in my head, I did manage to catch her as her rampage fizzled out. Leaving

my groceries behind, I remember picking her up, telling myself over and over to "Stay calm, just stay calm." Then I walked out of the store to my car. I reminded myself that I was truly in charge only of *my* behavior, that what other people said or thought was not as important as my relationship with my daughter, and that before I could even *think* of disciplining, I needed to release *my* frustrations and emotions safely! It took every parenting and self-management skill I had learned just to get through that event.

The skills you'll learn in this book won't make everything "perfect" in your world. They don't stop children from crying and they don't completely prevent scenes and challenging family situations. But they *will* help both you and your children to grow through each challenge, and to create relationships based on respect, cooperation, and unconditional love.

Today, I am happy to say, Arleigh is 13 years old and one of the most delightful people I know. I share that with you right from the start because so many parents have told me it brings them hope for their own situation. Dealing with a screamer can put the whole family into a tailspin and my family has certainly been there and back. You will, therefore, find lots of suggestions throughout this book for maintaining your sanity and for helping your child deal with her frustrations.

This book is not just for parents of screamers, however. One does not have to be in crisis or having problems to find this book helpful. It is a book for every parent who recognizes parenting as an important job in their life and who wants to ensure that their children have the skills and abilities to succeed and thrive in the years ahead. It is a book for every parent who wants to create a memorable, happy, and harmonious home life *right now*; and who wants to give their children the gift and strength of a respectful and loving relationship with the most important people in their lives – their parents.

Dorothy Corkille Briggs says that *the most important factor in determining healthy self-esteem in a child is the quality of relationship he has with significant others.* You, as parents, are the most significant people in your child's life. You are the experts in your own home.

"Expert" is a word that used to press every button I had – especially when it came to parenting. I used to think, "Who are they to tell me what to do in my own living room?" I highly recommend that you become very apprehensive and guarded about allowing *anyone* else to be the expert in your life. Take these words and ideas and bounce them against your own value system. If they fit for you, try them out. A word of caution, however: As you try these new approaches, the behavior you are trying to diminish may *at first* increase.

Think of it this way: My car used to go when I pressed this pedal, so what do I do if it doesn't go now? I press the pedal harder – and punch it down again. If children are used to pressing our buttons and getting a response, and now when they press there is *no* response, their natural inclination will be to press harder.

I recall sitting with a friend of mine as we were both learning these principles years ago. Her children were accustomed to her jumping up to meet their every demand. There we sat in her yard, with her daughter screaming and demanding her mother's attention inside – NOW! My friend was visibly twitching and quite distraught at *not* getting up to cater to her. However, with support, she held fast. Her daughter's fury and demands increased. Still, she held fast, as this was a pattern she knew she needed to change. Finally, her daughter came out to talk to her and they discussed the issue in the backyard.

This was not the only time such demands on her time arose, but my friend stuck to her resolution to respect herself and to help her children act more independently and respectfully towards her. Today, she counts her blessings that she did so. Once you decide to try a new technique or tool, stay with it and give it time to work.

There were many times when I was raising my children when I longed for them to "just hop to and do as I say when I say it." That never did happen, so this is not a book about how to turn your children into parent- or people-pleasing machines – regardless of how appealing that may seem in the heat of the moment!

No, this is a book about raising children who are full of spirit and life; about teaching them to be responsible, passionate, caring human beings who know who they are, what they want, and what they have to offer.

Think about the expectations you have in reading this book. I really don't believe I will be telling you anything you don't already know. My objective is to awaken and draw out that which is important to you and to give you some ideas and skills to put it into practice.

What do you want to get out of reading this book? Let go of any expectations you may have of becoming a "perfect parent." Let go of the idea of shaping the perfect child. Many power struggles and lasting battle scars are the result of parents trying to mold and shape their children into their idea of "perfect." Many parents have bent themselves into pretzels and have destroyed their own happiness and peace of mind trying to prove to the world that they are "perfect parents." So let "perfect" go and begin this book by welcoming mistakes. Mistakes are not only inevitable, they are essential to learning, growth, and success in life. Bill Gates was once asked, "How do I increase my rate of success?" His reply was simple: "Increase your rate of failure!"

You will make many "mistakes" as you read this book and you may find that some of the parenting principles and practices you've been using so far have not been to the greatest advantage of you or your children.

Be gentle with yourself! There is no point beating ourselves up for not having had these skills earlier. Berating and guilt-tripping ourselves are ways we use to divert or excuse ourselves from not using newly acquired skills.

Give yourself credit for investing your time and energy in the most important job in the world – parenting! In doing so, you are aligning your values with your actions. This is a huge stress reliever in and of itself.

Parents do the best they can with the skills that they have. Sometimes parents take on way too much responsibility for their children's behaviors. I believe children come to this world with built-in gifts, temperaments, and challenges. Sometimes even the best parenting skills cannot prevent children from "going astray." Perhaps our lesson in such situations is to let go of the guilt and to get a handle on our own thoughts and emotions. There is always an opportunity for us to learn in every situation. When we take that opportunity, we free our children to experience what they must, and to move through their lessons.

Whatever your situation is today, regardless of how difficult your relationship with your child is, you can still build a solid, loving, and cooperative relationship. It is never too late.

Begin using these tools and skills right *now*. Here. In this moment. Accept your situation fully, right now. Accept your children fully and know that even the most difficult child – *especially* the most difficult child – has a gift for you. She will help you find the strength, the patience, and the wisdom that lies within you and you will use every ounce of it to meet the challenges she creates. However, using it doesn't mean "using it up"! Patience, inner strength, and wisdom are like muscles – the more you use them the stronger you get, and yes, sometimes you have to feel the "burn" in order to build them further! My children have provided a regular workout schedule for me to develop those patience muscles. They have pressed every button I have and so I've discovered my buttons! *And* I have discovered how to stay in control of them, even in the midst of turmoil.

Gratitude is what I feel today toward my wonderful and spirited children. I set out looking for tools and techniques to help me change them – to mold them into the best people they could be. Instead of changing *them*, however, I changed *myself* and I learned how to encourage them to blossom into the wonderful people that they are. I found that the tools and techniques I learned in order to deal with these precious children that I love so much have been the most valuable tools and techniques I have ever put into practice for promoting my own personal growth and spiritual transformation. They are skills and tools I use in every relationship in my life, personally and professionally. They are tools and ideas that have allowed my family to sidestep the power struggles of the teen years, and to build a home characterized by respect, cooperation, and meaningful communication.

I have learned that parenting really has little to do with controlling my children and everything to do with controlling myself. Using power wisely in the parent-child relationship forms the foundation of this book. This is not easy, for when our children are small we need to do everything for them. Being able to step back and encourage them to do for themselves is a challenge. When I truly learned how to empower myself, I empowered my children. I discovered that when I give up the desire to control others, I gain the freedom to control myself and I grant my children the freedom to control *themselves*. And *that* has enriched my life and my relationship with my children a thousandfold.

So I offer you the tools, the insights, and the wisdom I have gained, not just from the experts who handed them down to me; not just from the hundreds of parents who attended my parenting classes; but from my children and from all children who have graciously consented to "teach" their parents, if the parent's mind is open enough. Take these tools and use them to enrich your own life.

The Way
of Mutual Respect

Cracking the old parenting mold

We get what we give.

*If you always do what you've always done,
you'll always get what you've always gotten.*

Respect. It's one of the cornerstones of being able to live life happily and successfully. Healthy relationships depend on it. Whenever I get together with a group of parents, it's one of their chief concerns: How do I teach my children respect? What's happened to the respect we used to know? Parents are often exasperated and discouraged over the lack of respect that they feel from their children.

"I just don't get it!" sighed one father in pure frustration. "I would never have *dared* to speak to my dad the way my son speaks to me! I'd have had that belt across my backside *so* fast... Yet I don't *really* want to use the belt – even if I wanted to, my wife wouldn't let me – so what can I do?"

"I know what you mean," empathized the woman sitting next to him. "I don't really want to raise my kids the same way I was raised. I mean, I don't want them to be *afraid* to speak up, but sometimes I'd rather *have* them afraid to speak up than speak to me the way they do. It's like I get no respect at all."

"Yeah, what's with that?" chimed in another man. "Whatever happened to respect anyway?"

Now isn't that the bottom line, I thought: *respect*. "So what does respect mean to you anyway?" I asked.

"Respect – treated with respect," replied one woman a little exasperatedly. "Like when I say something, they listen! They don't talk back; they don't question everything and treat me like I'm some sort of idiot."

"Yeah," added another, "and they help out around the house. Sometimes I think my kids expect me to do everything for them and yet they don't appreciate anything I do."

"Respect has a lot to do with being listened to," interrupted a dad. "When I was growing up, I listened to my dad; I had to! When he said 'Jump,' I asked, 'How high?'"

"So is this the bottom line?" I asked. "To be listened to? To be valued for our opinions – appreciated for our contributions to the family – recognized for our hard work?"

"Well, yeah, especially listened to and not argued with every step of the way. I mean, even if I didn't agree with my dad, I didn't argue with him. I didn't dare."

"Yeah, but did you respect him, or *fear* him?" asked one woman who'd been silent until now.

"Both," came the immediate response.

"I think the 'respect' we had for our parents was based on fear. That's what was expected. Parents controlled their kids through fear. That's not the kind of respect I want *my* kids to have for me. I don't want them to be afraid to question me, but I *do* want them to listen to what I have to say – and I want them to speak respectfully to me. I want them to help out when I ask them to, and to appreciate the things I work so hard to give them. But I don't want them to grow up afraid of me!" she ended emphatically.

A momentary silence spread throughout the room. This woman seemed to have put into words what all of us felt.

"So is there anybody who *doesn't* want that kind of respect?" I asked.

"Who *wouldn't* want that kind of respect?" replied one parent.

"What about our children?" I ventured. "Do you think *they* want that kind of respect?"

"Exactly," said the woman who'd spoken of fear and respect. "And I guess when we're talking about this kind of respect, we get what we give."

We get what we give

"We get what we give." That pretty much sums up the ideas, concepts, and tools you'll find in this book. We gain respect by respecting our children. I teach my children to respect my boundaries by setting clear boundaries and respecting theirs. When I respect their boundaries, I give them power to be able to respond to life situations. When I give them the space to claim *their* power, I get to claim *my* power. *We want powerful children who are respectful and responsible.*

Traditionally, society expected parents to control their kids and have power *over* them. This was interpreted as respect. As children, most of us accepted the belt across the backside and thought that one day *we* would be the parent. We expected that our children would accept *us* as the boss and authority in *their* lives. It is understandable that parents today feel frustrated, disappointed, and confused. Times have changed and today's children aren't willing to accept and respect us as the authority in their lives *just because* we are their parent.

This past century has seen the acknowledgment of human rights. We need only look at the labor movement, the women's movement, and the struggles of minority groups to be treated as people first. Is it any wonder that our children have joined the trend? They, too, want to be respected as people first.

Tradition can unite and connect us with our children, or it can keep us separate and trapped in roles that prevent us from truly knowing and respecting each other. Family rituals and gatherings provide a space for us to come together. When we use that space to get to know our children, tradition is a marvelous thing. Tradition reminds us that, as parents, we are indeed responsible for setting guidelines for our children. However, tradition can also divide us. If we get stuck in the roles, rules, and obligations of being the parent, and insist that our child play the traditional child's role, we may never actually get to know and truly unite with the most important people in our lives.

When we choose to view our children as people first, worthy of respect as human beings, we begin to see the many traditional beliefs in our society that have put children down.

§

MY TWO SONS, Jason and Tyler, were in their early teens when they decided to give each other an "artistic" haircut. One ended up with a "Mohawk"– a row of hair left standing in a single line all the way down the center of his head. The other preferred a "Bi-hawk" – *two* rows of hair making a double line across his head!

One day they were waiting for the bus when two women came and sat near them. "Look at those haircuts," chirped the first woman. "Can you imagine running around looking like that!"

"It's ridiculous," agreed the second woman. Then, turning to the clean-cut looking teenager sitting next to her, she said, "Not like you, dear. You're a nice clean-cut looking young man!"

Just then a bus pulled up and the two women stood up. As they were getting on the bus, one of them dropped some money. My son noticed and reached down to retrieve it. "Excuse me, ma'am," Tyler said to her as he handed her the money, "but you dropped this."

When she saw who was speaking to her, the woman's jaw dropped open and Tyler said she looked like she was going to fall over.

"Oh, thank you," stammered the woman, who then disappeared onto the bus.

As Tyler related this story to me, he said, "You know, Mom, it was like we were objects or something. They talked as if we had no feelings at all." Tyler also added that as soon as the bus pulled away from the stop the "clean-cut looking young man" lit up a cigarette!

⸎

Is it disrespectful if our kids want to wear their hair in a fashion that we consider outrageous? Or is it disrespectful to talk about people as if they aren't there?

Are the ways we have traditionally viewed children and their place in society helping us or hindering us? How do they affect our parenting practices?

Both parents and children are struggling to break free of the old parent-child mold. In the struggle to break the mold, the pendulum of change has sometimes swung so far that the kids are "running the show." Parents are left feeling powerless and disrespected, wondering "What went wrong?"

The key to breaking the mold is to stop playing the game of win-and-lose and embrace win-win. When I embrace win-win, I respect myself *and* my child. It is important as parents that we respect ourselves and let our children know, *respectfully,* when their behavior is out of line. In doing so, we teach other people how to treat us.

Show children you respect *your* time. Politely tell a complaining child that he is welcome to eat what he likes from the dinner selection, but that you are not making him a hot dog because that's "all he'll eat." Making the child his special dinner teaches the child he doesn't have to respect you and your time. Forcing him to sit and eat his broccoli crosses *his* boundaries and fails to respect *him.*

Setting a child down calmly and letting her know that you will not allow her to bite you shows respect for the child and for yourself. When we respect our child's boundaries *and* our own, we achieve a

> The key to breaking the mold is to stop playing the game of win-and-lose and embrace win-win.

win-win situation. This requires a new way of thinking about parenting and a whole new set of skills parents need to develop.

Traditional parenting gives parents license to cross their children's boundaries. We feel it is our *job* to cross those boundaries, but in our heart we don't feel good about it. That's why many parents have retreated from the traditional style of discipline. As we've retreated, however, we've allowed children to cross *our* boundaries. Children *do* need boundaries. Boundaries help them to feel safe. They provide healthy guidelines for their behavior. We set those guidelines by respecting both their boundaries and our own.

When we respect our boundaries, it teaches children how to behave in future relationships. A friend shared an amazing story that illustrates this point well.

§

BEFORE SHE WAS married, my friend visited her fiancé's home. She was alarmed to find her future mother-in-law still taking responsibility for getting her fiancé's 25-year-old brother out of bed and off to work. It took his mother half an hour of prodding just to rouse him from his nest.

Months later, after my friend had married, she was alarmed again to realize her husband expected *her* to get him out of bed to go to work. Months of struggle ensued, he blaming her for not getting him up in time and she insisting that this was not her job. Still, she found herself hooking in to getting him up.

Finally, she told him she would not be responsible and took action. She left her sleeping husband in the house as she drove off to work. That evening he was furious! He'd slept in and the principal of the school where he worked had called to wake him! The principal was not impressed.

"Oh, I'm sorry," my friend told her husband. "Do you want me to write a note to your principal explaining it was really not your fault as you expect your wife to get you out of bed?"

When she put it that way, her husband finally got it. Never again was she held responsible for getting him up!

§

Be aware that the relationship you create with your child establishes a pattern for his future relationships. It's important to empathize with our kids *and* to hold them responsible for their behavior and the impact it has on others. When we share our honest and heartfelt response to behavior that crosses our boundaries, it helps them to learn and understand how to get along with others.

§

CAROL'S ELDEST, MICHAEL, had just started university. Michael had worked hard all summer long: 14- and 16-hour days, seven days a week. The stress and strain of working and fixing the $375 truck he bought to travel to and from work was wearing on him. In truth, the whole family felt it. Carol hoped it would ease up when he started school. And it did, momentarily. Then, it built up again. Not only was his course load heavy and his truck in constant need of repair, but there were delays in cashing his Educational Savings Plan. Now it was October 6, his tuition was due on the 10th, and the money still wasn't in. On the 8th it finally arrived. Carol thought Michael would be relieved to see it and was looking forward to handing it to him. But Michael simply snatched it from her hand. He blamed the delay on the financial company the plan was purchased through. His only comment was, "It's about time – those morons!"

Carol was crushed. She had saved for years to put that savings plan together. This was not the scene she had envisioned at the moment of gifting. Michael had crossed her boundaries and she needed to convey that to him respectfully.

Carol waited for an appropriate time to talk. After dinner that evening she sought him out. Finding him alone, she shared her feelings with him.

"Michael, when you grabbed the check out of my hand like that this morning, I felt really crushed and disappointed. I worked hard to save that money. It was a gift and I need you to show some appreciation for it."

"Sorry, Mom," came Michael's reply, "but I can't believe they're such morons – do you know how stressful that was? I had to find a place to cash it today and rush to the cashier's at the college, and I still had a bunch of work to do in class."

"I hear how stressed you are, Michael, but being stressed doesn't give you a license to treat other people disrespectfully."

"But, Mom," Michael started to interject.

"No 'buts,' Michael," said Carol. "If you're stressed, it's up to you to do something about it. Spreading it to the people you live with will only drive the people you love the most away from you. Then you'll be even more stressed – and lonely!"

Michael plunked down with a sigh in a nearby chair. "Yeah, I guess you're right. But how do I deal with the stress? Sometimes it feels like someone started a race car up inside me and it's running full throttle, but it's hitting a wall and not going anywhere."

"That's stress all right," Carol empathized. "So is there anything that you can do that calms that racing inside?"

"Getting that check in earlier would have helped," said Michael.

"I agree, and you are usually pretty good at organizing things to do that. But in this case, that wasn't under your control. What *is* under your control is how you respond right now to the stress. For example, right now, do you still feel stressed inside?"

"Actually it's a bit better just talking about it," Michael replied.

"Great, so talking about it helps. What about breathing? Would you like to know a breathing technique that can calm you down on the inside?"

Michael was open to learning the technique so they spent the next few minutes practicing it. He said he felt better when they finished, gave his mom a hug, and told her again he really did appreciate the money for school. The entire family dynamics shifted right after that.

§

It takes skill and a different approach to parenting than we have traditionally taken to be able to convey our feelings in a way that is respectful and truthful. It means respecting our own boundaries and being willing to speak up when they are crossed. It also means respecting our child so that he can hear us without defensiveness. Few of us grew up with these skills. Be patient with yourself. It takes time and practice to develop them. Reading this book will help you develop and use the tools you'll need.

Parenting is a tough job, and every parent I've met knows it is their most important job. Parenting challenges us like nothing else. It presses all of our buttons, opens old wounds from our childhood, and the next thing we know, we hear our parents' words coming out of our mouths – the very words we swore we were never going to speak to our child! However, the words our parents used to silence us and to keep us in our place don't "work" with our children today.

This does not make the way that we were raised wrong. Our parents did the best they could, with the tools that they had, to meet the situations they were facing. We don't really want to silence our children, but we still want respect. We want our rights as parents acknowledged. And our children are demanding their rights.

Many parents tell me, "I don't want to raise my children the same way I was raised, but I don't know how to do anything else." There is a belief in society that parenting should just come naturally – like breathing! Some parents think, "Shouldn't I just be able to do what my parents did?"

I have a friend whose father and stepmother are raising their 13-year-old grandson. The young boy is regularly suspended from school for aggressive behavior. My friend's parents have refused parenting courses arguing that they *are* parents, so why do they need parenting courses? And didn't their daughter (my friend) turn out all right?
Yes, my friend *did* "turn out all right." In fact she's wonderful! But the skills they needed to raise *her* are not the skills they need *today*.

Today, there is rebellion and discontent sewn into the very fabric of society. The media and its influence are more prevalent in our homes than ever before. Children see violence, sex, and drugs everywhere, even when we're careful about monitoring television shows. Most of us no longer have extended family living in our household to help with the childrearing. Sometimes thousands of miles isolate us from any kind of family support. Many families have only one parent to support the children, and the stresses and pressures are many. However, all is *not* gloom and doom…

Parenting:
the "dangerous opportunity"

The Chinese character for crisis means "dangerous opportunity." Families *are* in crisis, but this is also a time of opportunity. It is a dangerous time, however, for it means leaving behind the old ways of controlling children through fear of punishment. Most people react to crisis by clinging to old, familiar ways, the ways that worked in the past. If we continue to focus on changing our children and the world outside of ourselves and do not take this opportunity to look within and to discover true power, the crisis will become more severe.

It takes courage to let go of the old and to welcome the new. The dangerous opportunity of parenting today requires us to let go of many of our traditional beliefs about parenting and to embrace a new and different kind of relationship with our child than most of us had growing up with our parents. There are many fine values and skills we learned from our parents and I value the many lessons my parents taught me. But my intention is that my children will grow and evolve well beyond me. So much of this will depend upon my ability to see and accept a different concept of power in the parent-child relationship.

The traditional parenting methods that no longer work today are those based on demanding respect through fear. The expectation that parents control their children, even if they must "break their spirit," still influences many parent-child relationships. Yet this is not in harmony with our goals. This means that we must let go of fear as a motivating force in shaping our child's behavior.

Most parents today seek a deep and meaningful connection with their child. This requires us to take a new look at the concept of power. The key is to stop resisting and to start embracing the changes. Instead of bemoaning the loss of "control" and "power" parents had, let us embrace the opportunity to develop relationships that empower us, and our children. Let's take advantage of the knowledge, understanding, and tools available for personal growth, and challenge ourselves to develop our full potential. We can invite our children to do the same. Our relationship with our children offers us a tremendous opportunity for personal and spiritual growth. So let's take that dangerous opportunity, dare to shift our perception of power, and create respectful, delightful relationships with our children.

> Our power as parents is not measured by our ability to control our children, but by our ability to empower them and ourselves.

Summary

Parenting today is very different from parenting years ago. Our whole idea of power and respect is changing. Perhaps it's time for a shift in the way we view children in our society. Respect is important to both parents and children. It's important to all of us! Respect means we acknowledge each other's boundaries. Effective parenting today means learning how to parent without crossing and disrespecting our children's boundaries. It also means teaching our children not to cross or disrespect *our* boundaries. This is a shift in the traditional methods of parenting. Times have changed and we as parents must change as well, as we rise to meet the challenges in this the most important work in our life – parenting. The changes and stress in our society have created a crisis for many families. Times of crisis provide great opportunity for growth.

2

The Way of Vision

Bringing Your Values to Life

Life is where we put our attention.
— RICHARD BACH

You must become the change you wish to see in the world.
— MAHATMA GANDHI

Whatever the mind and heart can conceive, you can achieve.

It's not the quantity of time spent with our children that is important but the quality.

Imagine you have $100 worth of energy pouring into you each day. Where are you investing it? If you are investing most of your energy and attention in your children's "acting out" behavior, their acting out behaviors will increase. If you are investing your energy in developing a healthy relationship, your relationship will flourish. Life goes where attention flows.

Simply becoming aware of where you invest your energy and attention will affect the environment in your home. The following questions serve as invaluable guidelines for developing the family atmosphere you really want.

Take a moment to relax and to reflect on your family's dynamics. Take an objective look at what goes on in your home and see if you can gage the barometric pressure:

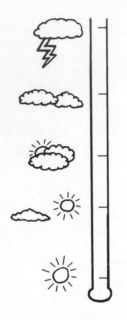

- How much communication in your home is in response to conflict? Do you wait for your child to misbehave before you give him your "intense attention"?
- How much communication is one-way directive, monologue communication? "Pick up your socks." "Put away your toys." "What's your jacket doing on the floor?"
- How often do you *seek out* your child's opinion?
- How completely do you listen to your child's opinions and feelings?
- How much time do you spend in *meaningful dialogue*?

Do not be discouraged if you just realized that the atmosphere in your home is not what you want it to be. Celebrate! Awareness is the first step. Make a note of where you are at now and return to this exercise once you've finished the book. Note any changes.

I can guarantee that the pressure will be on in your home if most of the communication is in response to conflict. One-way directives keep the atmosphere tense and stilted. Begin to seek out your child's opinion and listen when it's given, and the pressure will release substantially. A home characterized by meaningful dialogue provides a safe haven from the stresses of the world and empowers everyone to meet life's challenges.

Step back and *observe* the overall situation in your home. *Notice* the family patterns and group dynamics that exist. *Watch* the interaction between your children. *Notice* who is instigating situations. What is driving their behavior? *Become curious and observe all that you can.*

Bringing awareness to our situation is very powerful. Gathering accurate information is crucial. It helps us to center ourselves and keeps us from reacting negatively. After all, *life is where we put our attention!*

Creating a family vision

Creating a vision statement is a powerful and life-changing exercise. It will help you to

- define your deep and important values,
- keep your life and your relationship with your children in perspective and balance,
- make important decisions with confidence,
- discuss with your partner the kind of home you want,
- discipline from a position of depth and strength, and,
- provide focus and direction to your attempts to create a home where everyone can enjoy being together.

Maintaining balance and a sense of order in our homes is a big challenge for most parents. Step back from your life and take a moment to observe your style of parenting. When I first stepped back to observe what was happening in my family, I recognized that I was doing a lot of yo-yoing back and forth. On one hand, I wanted my kids to have fun, to enjoy themselves, and just be kids. On the other, I wanted to be in control. I didn't want them to have so much fun that they got on my nerves! I wanted them to listen to me.

One moment I'd be an easygoing, anything goes "jellyfish" parent, and the next moment I'd be reacting to my kids' misbehavior with a stiff-lipped raging "Major General" approach. After I'd raged for a while, I'd feel guilty; after all, I wanted them to like me, to visit me in my old age and to not "lose" my number. I wanted a meaningful relationship with my kids. So I'd return to the pleasing jellyfish role, letting their demands mold me. The goal of the jellyfish was to please the children and they knew it! And played upon it. The next thing I knew, I found myself stretched past my boundaries once again! Out comes Major General: "Parents are *supposed* to be in control, so listen up kids!"

Do you recognize yourself in either of these roles? Perhaps you see yourself in both of them. Do you favor one role and your partner takes the other? If one parent is the Major General, the other often takes the jellyfish role. Together they strike a rather precarious sort of balance. I say precarious because of the danger of becoming trapped in a deadlock, with each partner blaming the other for their unruly or overly stifled children. As long as one parent continues to blame the other, no one takes responsibility to create change and each becomes more entrenched in his or her own position. The whole family remains in a state of tension and reaction.

So how do we create what we want instead of reacting to what we don't want? The first step you've already taken. You've already seen yourself in the jellyfish/Major General model. You've noted when you're in a state of reaction. Continue to become aware of that reactive state. Simply noticing how our kids press our buttons helps us move out of that reactive state.

Taking things a step further, in *Conversations with God*, Neale Donald Walsch explains that if we want to move from *reaction* to *creation*, we need to look closely at the two words. Notice that the "c" has moved. To live a life of creation rather than reaction, we must see ("c") our life from a higher perspective. Lift yourself above *react*ionary patterns and begin to *create* what you truly want.

This is where the Family Vision Statement comes in. Put aside what is happening right now and *focus entirely on what you want to create.*

You cannot create what you cannot imagine. To help you create your vision, take time to complete the following exercise. This exercise gives direction to your life and your family. Do not allow limiting thoughts to enter by worrying about how you are going to create this vision. Just build it. You'll find the tools to create it in this book.

First, find a place where you can relax, undisturbed for the next 15 to 30 minutes. Close your eyes and take a few deep breaths.

Project yourself to your 90th birthday celebration. Imagine all of your children, your grandchildren, and your great-grandchildren gathered around you. Your children have prepared a speech to honor you and to thank you for the wonderful memories they have of growing up. They are going to talk about the tremendous foundation you have laid, not only for them, but also for the generations that have followed and for those that are yet to come.

- *Without limitation*, identify what you want them to remember.
- In vivid detail, write out *what you would like them to say*:
    - ~ What skills did they learn?
    - ~ What values have they inherited? What attitudes did they pick up from you?
    - ~ What words would they use to describe *you?*
    - ~ How do your children remember *you* behaving?
    - ~ What were the messages, both spoken and unspoken, that they received growing up with you?
    - ~ What do they remember doing together in your family?
    - ~ How did they feel about being together?

You have just summarized your deepest values and described what your family life would be like if you consistently acted on those values. The biggest step to creating that vision is to be the person you want to be, to act from that state of being. Then, you will have what you want.

At some point in our society, we adopted the belief that "When I have _____ (fill in the blank), then I'll be able to *do* _____ (fill in the blank) and then I'll be able to *be* _____ (what I've always wanted to be)!

For example, have you ever said to yourself, "When I *have* the time, I'll *play* (do) with my children and *then* I'll *be* the fun-loving mom

I've always wanted to be." Or what about this one: "When I *have* the patience, then I'll be able to *take the kids shopping* and *be the calm, tolerant, and loving kind of dad* I've always admired."

There is a major flaw in this belief system. Has anyone ever approached you and said, "Say, honey, it looks like you need some time, so here it is!" What about patience? Has anyone ever offered you patience? Of course not, because that isn't possible.

Let go of the have–do–be approach to life and embrace the approach that works: *Be–Do–Have, in that order!*

To activate your family vision and to create what you want in your life, begin with being. Feel *the emotion you want to prevail in your family and* act *from that emotion. Every time life is not going the way you want it to, remind yourself of what you want to be, feel yourself in that state, and then act from there.* If you do this consistently, with dedication and attention to the process, you will eventually have what you want because you will create it. Remember: the power and the time to create is always right *now*, starting from being.

Steven Covey, in his acclaimed book *Seven Habits of Highly Effective People*, uses a slightly different approach to building this vision. He suggests that to make this vision more immediate and to really drive you to live from the heart of what's most important in your life, imagine yourself six months from now – at your own funeral. Again, what would you want your children to say? How about your partner/spouse?

This may feel awkward or even harsh, but if you do this exercise in earnest you will begin living your life from your deepest values. Challenge yourself to live the next six months as if they were your last. Make each moment count and strive to live the way you have just described as ideal. You will live a life of creation, not reaction.

Do not worry about the discrepancy between where you're at right now and where you want to be. Feel and fully accept where you are at right now. Then set the vision in motion by sending out the *intention* for it to occur. *Detach* from your desire to know exactly *how* it will come about. You cannot plan each step of the way. This detachment is crucial, or you may frustrate yourself and those around you by trying to bend people to fit your vision. Let go. Focus on right now. Fully accept where you are. Accept your children and your partner as *they* are right now. Stop questioning if you're on the right track. Of course you're on the right track! Where you are right now is the only place you can be!

Now, in this moment, start to look for evidence of your vision taking shape. When your children are getting along, drink it in! Notice it! Feed it your attention. You will start to notice more and more things that are working in your life because you are looking for them.

Feel the emotion you want to prevail in your family and act from that emotion. Look for the qualities you *want* to see in your family. Search for and find even the smallest hints of those qualities and give them your attention. Remember that we tend to find what we expect to find.

Have you ever noticed how you see pregnant women everywhere when you or your partner is pregnant? Or Mazdas everywhere you look, as soon as you think about buying a Mazda? We tend to find what we're looking for, *so search for and comment on the positive behaviors you want to see.*

Stay centered in the now, holding your vision. "Don't sweat the small stuff." Always remind yourself to stay present, in this moment. Remember that "life is where we put our attention."

Of course, you may still feel yourself gravitating from jellyfish to Major General, but now you've added another dimension. You have a deeper force working to create the life you want. Instead of being tossed about reacting to your children's *behavior*, you're acting from your *values*.

On your own or with your partner, continue to build and create the vision for your family, and practice holding that vision in your mind and heart. Act from that vision.

Involving your children in the process

You can ask your children to join you in creating a family vision. However, children sometimes become suspicious or refuse to take us seriously if we suddenly ask them to join us in creating this vision.

It's often better to create the vision *first* and to bring our actions into alignment with it. That way we gain credibility and trust with our children.

Speaking personally, this was certainly something that *I* needed to do before I asked the rest of the family to join me in creating a vision.

§

JUST LIKE I NOW RECOMMEND parents do, I had spent time describing in detail the family and home that I wanted to have, focusing primarily upon my role as mother: I was calm, centered, patient, and encouraging. I learned from my mistakes and allowed my children to do the same by always focusing on solutions. I was inspirational in how I lived my own life; I was caring and sensitive; I was able to have fun with my kids, laughing and giggling and not getting too uptight about the "small stuff," while staying centered and productive. The list went on and on. I painted a vivid picture of what I wanted to create and vowed to keep my actions in line with this vision. The trick was to stay in the moment and to *consciously* bring all of those qualities into it.

Well, have you ever noticed how "the moment" has a way of getting away from you? Have you ever gotten so swept up into the drama of the day that you lose sight of the day…and of your vision for it? That's pretty much what happened to me one sunny Sunday afternoon.

It was a gorgeous spring day and families everywhere were in their backyards raking and digging and playing. I myself was headed down to the haystack in the orchard to enjoy a glass of wine with my sister-in-law in the late afternoon, when I noticed my two sons and their cousin sitting happily on a rather distant pile of bales. I smiled – they looked so happy and industrious – and then I noticed glimpses of silver flashing out around their hands. Alarmed, I hurried over to see what was going on.

"Hey, Tyler," I called to my four-year-old as I approached. "What are you doing?"

"Nothing," Tyler sang in a muffled kind of voice, refusing to look up at me.

Oh-oh, that meant something was up. And then I saw it. My four-year-old had a jackknife in his hand! "Tyler! What are you doing with that knife!" It really wasn't a question – more of an alarmed exclamation.

Tyler didn't even look up. "Whittowing," came the simple reply.

"Not even able to say the word, and he has a jackknife in his hands," I muttered under my breath. I was sprinting toward him now: "Tyler, give me that knife! You'll hurt yourself!"

But Tyler immediately pulled it away from my reach. "Daddy said I could have it."

"What?" My jaw dropped open in amazement. Just at that moment his father rounded the corner of the shed. I gave him one of *those* looks. "Tyler says you gave him that jackknife."

"Yeah, so?"

"Lou, he's only four years old! He'll hurt himself."

"He'll be all right, Maggie – relax! You're always over-reacting."

"Relax! Okay sure," I said sarcastically, my defenses now completely taking over. Here we go again, I thought, and like a tire sliding into a well-worn track, I slid right into the age-old argument with my husband. "Relax! Oh yeah, sure! A four-year-old with a jackknife and you want me to relax."

"He'll be all right, Maggie!"

How I hated fighting in front of the kids, especially when it made me out to be the uptight worrywart. I looked at the three boys and at my husband all defending their manly right to use a jackknife and knew this was a battle I could not win. Still, the sight of blood – even the *thought* of an open wound – made me squirm and wince inside. "Well if he cuts himself, you better be here to deal with it!" I gave it my parting shot and went to join my sister-in-law on her set of bales.

She gave me a sympathetic look and offered me a glass of wine. We jumped right into conversation and I forgot all about the boys and their jackknives, until a blood curdling scream ripped through the air. Instantly, I knew what had happened. Panic-stricken, I raced toward my young son. I could see blood dripping from his hand.

"Lou!" I screamed as I ran. "Lou! Where are you anyway?" I raged. "Lou!" By this time I had reached Tyler. This was exactly what I had predicted. A bleeding kid and I had to deal with it. "I told you you'd cut yourself," I admonished Tyler. "What did I tell you? And where is your father now," I continued, as I half lifted and half dragged Tyler toward the house. "Gone! Nowhere in sight! Didn't I tell you this would happen…" On and on I raged as I "escorted" Tyler to the house.

Suddenly, something inside me woke up and I saw myself from a higher perspective. It was almost as if I left my body and looked down to see this raging madwoman dragging a terrified little boy down a dusty orchard path. "*This,*" said a voice inside, "is patient, calm, caring, open to learning from mistakes?" The vision of the mother I wanted to be clicked in and instantly I changed my behavior. "Oh yeah," I told myself, "Calm down," and taking a deep breath, I relaxed. "Accept the moment," I continued to coach myself. "Be here now. This is a learning opportunity."

I looked down at Tyler. He was stark white and looked like he hardly dared to breathe. Patience and compassion flooded through me. "Breathe, honey, it's okay," I said in a soothing voice. Tyler looked up at me in disbelief. *This was the same mother who had been raging only a moment before?* "It's okay, honey," I said again. "We'll have this fixed up in no time. Sorry I overreacted," I added. "Take a deep breath and relax…"

We walked calmly, almost serenely the rest of the way to the house. Once we got there, we ran some cleansing water over his hand and talked about the amazing healing power of his body, including the many healing forces that were gathering together to stop the bleeding. Together, we got the first-aid kit out and bandaged his finger. Soon his wound would heal and he wouldn't even be able to see where he had cut himself.

⸙

A Course in Miracles says that "a miracle is a shift in perception." That day, I experienced a miraculous shift in perception firsthand. My sister-in-law was astounded when Tyler and I emerged from the house almost in a state of grace. "You two are like a different couple from the two people I saw going up to the house," she told us. Indeed, by that point, I *felt* like a totally different person from the raging lunatic who had reacted to the accident. By shifting my perception and by adopting the vision of who I wanted to be, I created an experience that reflected my deepest values.

This experience turned out to be a demonstration of learning from mistakes and of how to remain calm. It was a tremendous bonding opportunity for me and my son. And on top of that, we threw in a little biology lesson! *What power we wield when we choose to create what we want rather than react to what we don't want!*

I worked at creating and building my *own* vision of how I wanted to be in my family for quite some time, before I invited my family to sit down and join me in creating a vision together. Then, one evening, I said to everyone (my two boys, six and eight years old; my three-year-old daughter; and my husband) "I want everyone to think about what would make our home the best place in the world to be. After supper I want to talk about it."

I knew that it would be important to have everyone's input, even that of my three-year-old, and with this in mind I called the family together. We all sat around the table.

"I've noticed that lately there's been quite a bit of arguing and fighting going on around here – with all of us – and a bit too much yelling, too," I began. "I don't see that you kids are very happy with all of this fighting and yelling. None of us are. You know, this is the only home we have. Wouldn't it be great if it was the best home in the world? What do you think, guys?"

"Well, yeah, but it's not," quipped my oldest.

"Well, who do you think could make it that way?" I asked. I looked at the boys and continued, "Fighting and arguing becomes a bad habit that doesn't end just because you leave here. It's a habit you'll carry with you. *Now* is the time to create the life that makes us all happier. We're the only ones who can do that. *We* decide what kind of home we live in. What ideas did you think of to help us create the best home possible?" The kids looked a little puzzled. "How would we treat each other if this were the very best place in the world to be?" I prompted them.

Finally Tyler piped up: "We'd treat each other like friends."

"And how do friends treat each other, Tyler?" I asked.

"They say things they like about each other."

I wrote it down. "What else?"

"Friends are honest and they don't yell at each other."

I wrote down "honesty," and wanting to phrase it positively, "speak in normal tones." (That soon got shortened to "Don't yell!")

"What else do friends do?" I asked.

"Have fun," said my three-year-old.

I wrote it down. We continued discussing how friends treat each other and building our list. When it was finished, I asked if it would be a good idea if I wrote it out again and posted it on the fridge – that way, we could all remind each other of the guidelines we had chosen to make our home the best it could be. Everyone agreed and that Vision Statement stayed on our fridge for years. I've copied it here simply as an example of something you might want to try. Of course, you will have your own ideas and words.

Our Family Vision
Friends in Our Family

Honesty Respect Love

- look for & say things we like about each other
- do & say what we really believe is right – listen to our spirit-God
- speak in normal tones
- keep our environment orderly
- all work to clean up the house
- use our sense of humor
- look out for each other
- listen to each other without interrupting
- keep our word
- settle arguments peacefully
- celebrate! have fun, appreciate each other
- don't embarrass, ignore, or contradict one another

Building a Family Vision Statement has been one of the most powerful and influential exercises that I have ever done with my family. Whenever one of us yelled, someone was quick to remind us of our agreement: "No yelling." When the kids felt that they had a say in enforcing guidelines that made their life more pleasant, they were more ready to cooperate with the guidelines that made *my* life easier, such as "let's clean up now." Adherence to our family vision brought to life the ideas we've been discussing about respect and power.

When you're ready to get together with your family to create your own vision, here are a few hints to keep in mind.

- Create your own vision first and work with it to bring it to life.
- Timing is very important. When you invite your family to create a vision together, choose a time and place that is good for everyone.
- Keep it positive and light. Focus on "What would it take to make our home the very best place in the world to be?" Do not allow it to become a blaming session.
- Write down everyone's ideas and use the children's words as much as possible.
- Be prepared to live by the guidelines.
- Make it clear that some guidelines will be different for parents than for children. Parents still make the final decisions about health and safety issues and, of course, they will not have the same bedtime as their children!

Summary

The choice of where we put our attention can change our life. Congratulate yourself if you have increased your awareness of your family dynamics. Keep the communication barometer in mind as you interact with your family. Give less attention to conflict, seek out your children's opinions, and create meaningful conversations.

Notice and give attention to what's working right now in your family. Create a clear vision of what your home would be like if everything were just the way you want it. Imagine vividly how *you* would act if your home were perfect and let that be your guide as you interact with your children. Review your vision often. When your family is ready, you can invite them together to build a vision and develop guidelines for your entire family.

3

The Way of
Mutual Empowerment

Turning Power Struggles
into Powerful Relationships

The passion for setting people right is in itself an afflictive disease.

*When I give up the desire or need to control you,
I gain the freedom to control myself.*

True power lies behind the eyes.
— CAROLINE MYSS

§

EMILY STORMS IN the door from school, slamming it
shut behind her. Her mother hears the door slam shut and
automatically responds, "Emily, how many times do I have
to tell you, don't slam the door!" Then she looks up just in
time to see Emily giving the cat a good, swift boot. "Emily!
Don't hurt the cat! What do you think you're doing, young
lady? Go to your room immediately!"

Emily simply stares back at her mom defiantly and stomps up the stairs, giving her little brother a shove along the way.

Mother rushes over to rescue her crying son. "Emily!" Mother's voice has risen considerably in volume and her face is flushed with anger: "How *dare* you hurt your brother – he didn't do anything to you! Now go to your room and stay there."

"No!" screams Emily. "You can't make me!"

"You get to your room this minute, young lady, and don't even think about coming out before suppertime."

"No!" Emily screams again, but turns and races down the hall away from her mother who is heading toward her, little brother in tow. Emily runs into her room, slamming the door as hard as she can behind her.

"How dare you slam your door," Mom yells through the wall at her, but her daughter's screaming is her only response. Angry and exhausted, Mom heads back to the living room.

§

Power struggles often result from parents trying to change their child's behavior. When our child acts out, we want to move in and *stop* it. The problem is that we run into resistance. Our child digs in her heels, we dig in ours, and the struggle for power is on!

Mom did not like Emily's behavior and felt it was her job to make Emily change it. Mom, operating from a faulty parenting belief, thought that if she made Emily feel bad, Emily would act better. But has Mom achieved this?

Do you think for a minute that Emily is sitting in her room trying to figure out how she can change her behavior to please her mother and brother? Not likely! Chances are great that she's feeling even more miserable than when she first came through the door and she may well be plotting her revenge.

After Mom settles her son and settles down herself, she may feel disappointed and hurt or even guilty. After all, she was looking forward to spending some quality time with her daughter. Still, she couldn't let her get away with slamming the door, kicking the cat, and pushing her brother, could she?

Mom and Emily got caught in a power struggle familiar to all parents. But how did it happen in the first place?

The circle of empowerment

Let's look at what happened in light of a model I call The Circle of Empowerment. This model has been effective in my parenting classes because it demonstrates how to get out of power struggles. It helps parents to see the pattern they get locked into in relationships. It shows how we can empower our children and ourselves by fully claiming our own power and by allowing our children to claim theirs. It outlines boundaries and demonstrates how we can increase our child's self-esteem as well as our own, and can enjoy a lifelong relationship based on respect and love. People have found this model to be effective in every relationship in their life. For simplicity's sake, I will put Emily and Mom into the model.

The Circle of Empowerment

Emily's Emotions

Emily's Behavior

Mom's Emotions

Mom's Reaction

Emotions power behavior. If Emily had been feeling good about herself when she came through the door, she probably wouldn't have slammed it. Notice how this scenario starts with Emily's emotions, which lead to Emily's behavior, which affects Mom's emotions and generates her reaction or behavior, which affects Emily's feelings, and so on. The cycle moves clockwise and is replayed again and again, gaining in intensity and speed. Let's look at what happened again, step by step.

- *Emily's emotions and feelings* drive her behavior. She comes through the door feeling lousy.
- *Her behavior* reflects her feelings. She slams the door.
- Emily's behavior *annoys her mother*.
- *Mom reacts* from her emotions and yells at Emily.
- Mom's reaction *intensifies* Emily's already negative feelings.
- Emily now feels worse and *she acts out again by kicking the cat*.
- Now *Mom is really annoyed* and adopts the "young lady" voice.
- Mom feels she must teach Emily how to behave. *She focuses her attention on making Emily change her behavior*.
- *Emily's frustration increases* when she feels her mother's attempts to change her behavior.
- Naturally, *Emily resists and intensifies her offensive behavior* by shoving her baby brother.
- This *presses "Mama Bear's" buttons* big time.
- *"Mama Bear" reacts swiftly*, rescuing her son and sending her daughter to her room.
- *Emily feels even more frustrated* and perhaps even *jealous* of her brother for receiving her mom's attention.
- *Emily refuses* to go to her room.
- Mom feels Emily *challenge* her authority.
- Mom moves to *make* Emily go.
- Emily is *frightened* and even more *frustrated* and *agitated*.
- Acting out her frustration, Emily *slams* the door to her room shut.
- Mom is *annoyed* and feels *challenged* again.
- Again *Mom tries to correct her daughter's behavior* by lecturing her about the door.
- *Emily feels isolated and frustrated* and may well be plotting her revenge.
- And the vicious cycle continues.

The struggle may continue for days, but it could last for a lifetime. Round and round they go, Mom focusing on changing her daughter's behavior, and Emily, angry at being pushed, pushing back and intensifying her negative behavior.

Let's step back from this cyclone for a moment and see what is happening in terms of power dynamics.

Neither Mom nor Emily feels as if she has any power. Mom is using all of her power to try to change her daughter and Emily is using all of her power to resist her mother. Their power is tied up in pushing against each other. No wonder they are in a power struggle, for each person is literally grasping for power.

As long as Mom remains focused on controlling Emily, she will always be locked in the power struggle. Mom thinks it is her job to control her daughter and that when she controls her daughter she will have power in the relationship. (This is why I said earlier that traditional parenting gave us a license to cross children's boundaries. Parents focused on changing their child's behavior because they were expected to do so.) But Mom is not using her power appropriately and will actually prevent her daughter from understanding and using her power.

Whenever our intention and focus is on changing someone else's behavior we have crossed their boundaries. We can influence and guide our children's behavior best by respecting their boundaries and by focusing on changing our own behavior. *Now* we are claiming our *true* power, allowing our child to claim hers, and the shift in the relationship will create change in our child's behavior.

Let's take another look at the circle to see where *true* power lies:

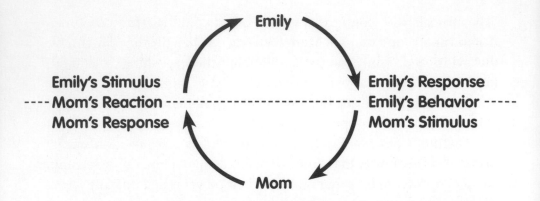

If we draw a line horizontally through the circle, we set up healthy boundaries for both Mom and Emily. In reality, each only has power to influence behavior on their side of the line. As well, for both Mom and Emily, *true power lies in the gap between stimulus and response, and in realizing that the only person's behavior you can control is your own.* Emily's behavior becomes Mom's stimulus for taking action and Mom's reaction or response to Emily's behavior becomes Emily's stimulus.

As before, the circle moves clockwise. When Mom focuses on changing Emily's behavior instead of focusing on what action *she herself* will take, she sets the circle spinning. She misses the opportunity to take full advantage of her own power. Emily feels the pressure and instead of focusing on changing her *own* behavior (and thus using her power), she pushes back.

The vicious cycle begins to spin faster as they spiral into the center.

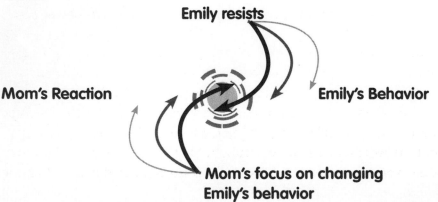

See how small the gap is now between stimulus and response? That's why neither one of them feels they have any real power.

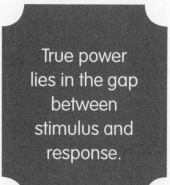

True power lies in the gap between stimulus and response.

So how do they break this deadlock?

The good news is that the solution is quite simple, though it is not always easy to carry out. *When* either one *of them recognizes that she's struggling, she must let go. That's it. Stop struggling; pause; and step back from the power struggle.*

So how does one "step back" from a power struggle?

One way to let go of the struggle is to notice your body's tension and to let go physically first.

- Check your posture. Are you tensed, leaning forward?
- Is your jaw clenched, or your fists? Is your stomach tight?
- Have you stopped breathing? (Continuing to breathe is important!)

Noticing and changing your physical posture can free you and your child from power struggles. Stand up straight, take a step back, breathe deeply, and relax tensed muscles.

The freeze-frame technique presented in the book *The HeartMath Solution* describes how you can calm your entire system and bring your emotions, thoughts, and physical body into alignment, by focusing your attention on your heart and by "breathing" through it. Then, you allow yourself to feel the peace you want to feel right now by recalling a situation from the past where you felt peaceful. Next, ask your heart for advice in this situation. (For a more complete description of this method, see *The HeartMath Solution*, by Doc Childre and Howard Martin, with Donna Beech, HarperSanFrancisco, 2000.)

It also helps to check our mental response. We can coach ourselves by reminding ourselves to "Let go, just let it go," or "Relax, just relax." Find the words, or the inner dialogue that works best for you. What would you say to someone else to help them calm down and end a power struggle? Often, what we'd tell others is exactly what we need to tell ourselves. Whatever you tell yourself, remember: *True power has nothing to do with controlling someone else and everything to do with controlling oneself.*

> True power has nothing to do with controlling someone else and everything to do with controlling oneself.

One parent called this moment of pausing and stepping back to take power over her own actions the "power pause." She liked it and it worked so well she taught her children to "take the power pause."

What if Mom decides to take the power pause and stops struggling? Emily has nothing to push against. If Emily wants her mom's attention, she may try harder to push her buttons, but if Mom continues to claim her power and to focus on the question "What will *I* do?" Emily can't push them unless Mom lets her.

You may be right!

Beware of the need to be "right" in your relationship with your children. In the scenario with Mom and Emily, Mom may feel it is her *job* to be right! If Mom has to be right, then someone has to be wrong, and in this case that someone is Emily! However, Emily doesn't want to be wrong, either.

"You may be right" is a powerful phrase that can immediately end a power struggle. It gives both parties space to reconsider their position. It allows both to let go and stop pushing.

§

A FRIEND INTRODUCED me to this phrase years ago. She'd just come from a parenting class and she said, "You know, I'm going to see if this works with Dan – he and I are always at loggerheads." She didn't have long to wait.

That night as her 12-year-old son was setting the table, they started into a typical argument. As soon as Jayne realized she was in a power struggle, she straightened up, relaxed, and said, "You know what, Dan, you may be right." Silence. Dan stopped arguing immediately. Jayne enjoyed peace and quiet all through dinner.

As Jayne was doing the dishes that night, she started to think about how magically "You may be right" had ended their power struggle. And then she started to think, "You know what? He *may*, actually, *be* right. Ah! He *is* right!"

When she gave herself the space to consider that Dan might be right, she let go of her need to be right and opened up to new possibilities. She told me it was a wonderful lesson in how she closed down her own thought processes with the need to be right. She also started to realize how much needless energy she spent in power struggles.

§

Stop judging

Those are some tools to help Mom end the power struggle. However, Mom and Emily still have a problem because of Emily's agitation when she came home and slammed the door.

Mom is operating from generations of programming that taught parents it is their job to be right and to teach children to act appropriately. Parents *do* need to guide children to understand what constitutes appropriate behavior. However, *we can get so involved in correcting our child's behavior that we destroy our relationship with them.*

Parents often believe they need to judge whether their child's behavior is good or bad, and reward or correct them accordingly. But *it is this very judgment that closes relationships down and throws them into turmoil.*

When you feel judged, don't you close down and become defensive? How many adult relationships have you been in where being judged and corrected all the time, or needing to judge and correct your partner, has been a source of problems? Why would it be any different with our children?

Still, it is not easy to stop judging. Sometimes you end up judging whether or not you're judging! In my own life, when I recognized how much I judged my partner and my children, I became quite miserable because I did not understand how I could stop. It had become a habit – albeit an uncomfortable one. Then one day someone said to me *"Whenever you catch yourself making a judgment, turn that judgment into curiosity!"*

Bingo! That concept revolutionized my relationship with my children. Instead of judging their behavior and feeling that I needed to correct it, curiosity opened the door to helping my children release their frustrations and other emotions.

Understanding that emotions drive behavior, I began to welcome the healthy release of those emotions. "Oh yeah," I'd say to myself, "I wonder what's bothering him?" I no longer needed to make the emotion wrong. My new attitude created a safe space for my kids to open up and release the emotions driving the behavior. Most of the time, the behavior then settled naturally. Their main need was simply to express the emotion and be heard. Of course, there were many times I'd catch myself in the power struggle first, before remembering to turn my judgments to curiosity, but it became easier as time went on and I found myself having fewer and fewer struggles as I let go of the need to control my kids.

What if Mom had turned her judgment of Emily's behavior to curiosity? Instead of trying to correct Emily and to get her to change her behavior, what if she'd have thought to herself, "Whoa, I wonder what's bothering her today?" Aloud Mom might say, "Hey, honey, you really seem upset. What's up?"

Notice what Mom did here. She shifted her perception of Emily's behavior by changing judgment to curiosity, and she chose to *respond* rather than *react*. It's important that Mom's question is genuinely open and curious. "What's the matter with you today?" spoken in an annoyed tone of voice will only create defensiveness and set them both spinning toward a power struggle.

Shifting perception and letting go of judgment takes conscious effort and practice and Mom may fall into her old patterns many times before she catches herself at the beginning and completely avoids the power struggle. However, *Mom can catch herself at any point in the interaction. If she finds herself in a power struggle, all she need do is let go and calm down. Her primary focus is to manage her own inner environment, to remind herself of her highest vision of who she wants to be, and to act from that state of being. Her curiosity and her desire to help her daughter release frustration will direct her actions.* If she stays focused on, "What will I do now?" she will give her daughter room to claim her power and focus on her behavior.

Increasing self-esteem

When we give children the space to claim their own power, we automatically increase their self-esteem. Self-esteem is the belief we have about who we are and the abilities we possess. People with high self-esteem know their own personal power and use it to expand their abilities and skills. They are not concerned about what someone else will make them do or what they need to make others do. *They* decide what they will do! As mentioned in the Introduction, author Dorothy Corkille Briggs tells us that the most significant influence on a child's self-esteem is the quality of the relationships she has with significant others. Parents are a child's most "significant others."

I used to call the Circle of Empowerment the Circle of Self-Esteem because if Mom and Emily spend too much of their time and energy struggling for power it will wear away at the self-esteem of both of them. If Mom focuses on empowering herself and encouraging Emily to claim her true power, both of them will increase their self-esteem. They are interconnected. If Emily continues to feel frustrated and angry, she will continue to act out. If Mom continues trying to change Emily's behavior, *she* will feel frustrated and angry. She will begin to doubt her ability as a parent. As Mom's self-esteem sinks, her behavior will deteriorate. Acting from desperation in her attempts to change her daughter's behavior, she may either propel Emily into intense rebellion or Emily will quietly turn against herself. Either way, neither one of them feels good about herself.

Before I learned to respect my children's boundaries, I set myself up for frustration and failure. I had little self-esteem, feeling like I was failing with my children. And my kids didn't feel very good about themselves, either. However, when I started to focus on what *I* would do, not on what I needed to make *them* do, we all felt better about ourselves and our relationships deepened and grew.

I kept the idea of being curious about my children foremost in my mind and I started to get to know them; to understand who they truly are, what their interests are, what hidden abilities they have. *I let go of trying to shape them into who I thought they should be and watched with excitement and curiosity as the person inside emerged. And I was able to let go of the desire and the need to control them. In doing so, I gained the freedom to control myself.*

Being non-judgmental is essential to building trust. This is a powerful concept to put to work in *every* relationship. Recently, I visited friends who had just returned from an intensive workshop on healing marriage issues. On their fridge was a reminder to "Turn judgments into curiosity!"

Stop letting your child press your buttons!

Avoid reacting and choose your actions. Take the "power pause" and stay focused on "What will *I* do" rather than on "What do I need to make my *child* do?"

- If your child is having a screaming fit in the store, don't try to *make* her stop screaming; focus on calmly carrying her out of the store.
- If your child won't get dressed, don't try to *make* him; let him know when you're leaving and that, if he's not dressed, he'll go to preschool in his pajamas. If he's not dressed when the time comes, focus on carrying him calmly to the car or bus in his pajamas. Avoid lecturing and trying to make him feel bad.
- If your teenager speaks rudely to you, focus on what you will do, not on what you will make her do. You may simply choose to walk away at this point rather than hook into a struggle. Gather

your thoughts and deal with it later. In chapter 5 we'll explore a tool to help you express yourself and your needs without creating defensiveness in your children.

- If your child refuses to help with dishes, don't try to *make* her do them. Leave the dishes, telling her the next meal will be made after she does them. Or tell her you'd be happy to drive her to her friend's *after* she's done the dishes.

These solutions may sound simple, but it often takes a lot of resolve and determination just to carry through with them. Remember that we are breaking through deeply ingrained habits and parenting concepts that would have us focus on changing our child's behavior, not our own. The following story demonstrates the inner battle we can go through when we put this philosophy into action.

§

"UGH!" SIX-YEAR-OLD AMBER grunted with disgust. "I *hate* these gloves. I *hate* skiing! Why did we have to come here?"

"Next," the chairlift attendant probed us to move on.

"Come on, honey," Fran said. "We can fix your gloves when we're on the lift." Wearily Fran pulled her reluctant daughter toward the lift. What was the matter with this picture? Wasn't this supposed to be *fun*?

The chair attendant stepped forward to help Amber onto the lift, but Amber scowled at him like a mother wolf defending her cubs and growled, "I can do it *myself!*" Wisely, the attendant backed off without a word and Amber and her mom were whisked away on the chair. Funny how nobody else wanted to ride up with them, isn't it? Not even Amber's brothers dared to join them. They were following on the next chair. No way were they going to be caught up there with their sister's bad mood sitting next to them!

Amber sulked and sputtered and fumed all the way

up the lift. Fran tried hard to maintain a positive, cheery attitude, despite her growing annoyance and impatience. "I am the adult here," she reminded herself. "I have 39 years' experience on this planet and I will not allow a six-year-old to dictate my moods and ruin my family day out skiing."

Experience had taught Fran there was no point in arguing with Amber – it only added fuel to Amber's fire. Reasoning hadn't worked very well either. How does one reason with a six-year-old determined to hang on to her misery, anyway? Today she appeared out to destroy any happiness and good cheer her mother might have as well. Fran had to keep reminding herself, "I choose how I feel; nobody else can make me feel anything; I choose how I feel. I decide what I will do; I don't need to make her do anything. All I have to concentrate on is what I will do." On and on Fran steadied herself in her own mind. "So she can sit and fume if she likes. I will enjoy myself. I will not get caught up in her misery, or in my need to fix her misery. We know that doesn't work!"

Fran had spent far too much time in the past wearing herself out trying to please her daughter and to avoid her ultimate weapon – scream torture. Learning to focus on what Fran would do rather than trying to change her daughter's behavior had not been an easy lesson. It was, however, the one thing that helped her maintain her sanity and she was determined to make "What will I do" the focal point of her day today.

"Mom," Amber's voice shook Fran out of her reverie. "Aren't you listening to me? I hate these gloves, why do I have to wear them?"

"I can see you're frustrated with trying to get them to fit your hand properly," Fran kept her voice even and patient. "Would you like some help with them?"

"No! I hate them! Why do I have to wear them?"

"Well it's your choice whether you wear them or not, dear." It's possible the "dear" part sounded a little strained. "I just think your hands may get cold without them. But it is your choice." Fran had learned years ago that the natural consequence of being cold convinced Amber to wear gloves more readily than anything Fran could say. Reminding Amber that she had choices and power to decide for herself also helped ease the strain in these difficult moments.

"Oh, here we are at the top of the lift," Fran noted with some relief. "Ready to get off, Amber?"

"I guess so," came the reluctant reply. Clearly there was not much of an alternative.

They skied off and stopped to wait for the boys. Fran offered again to help Amber straighten her gloves, but Amber started grumbling again, so Fran just left her to herself. "Focus on what I will do," Fran kept coaching herself. It seemed like a simple enough statement, but in the past Fran had experienced difficulty in following through. Amber's whining and wailing usually got to her and she ended up doing just about anything to please her.

"Here are the boys, Amber. Ready to ski down?"

"No! Don't want to."

"That's fine, dear, it's up to you." Again Fran reminded herself to let natural consequences be the teacher here. After all, where else could Amber go? "Okay, Amber, we're off. We'll ski down to that grove of trees right there and wait for you." And without another word, Fran and the boys skied off. "Free at last!" thought Fran.

Before she'd even reached the trees, Amber's plaintive wail rang across the mountainside. "M-o-o-o-o-o-o-o-o-o-o-o-o-m-m-m! Get back here!"

Fran smiled to herself. Sorry dear, this time I really can't. Not even if I was tempted to. Not surprisingly, it didn't take Amber long to reach them. Fran greeted her warmly, and they carried on down the hill in the same manner, with Fran skiing just slightly ahead of Amber, all the way to the bottom.

With no one to argue with and no one to fix things for her, Amber eventually straightened out her gloves, and herself, and by the time they reached the bottom her mood had shifted. Out came the delightful child they all loved to be with.

Fran congratulated herself on not hooking into an all-day argument with her daughter. She also sent out a prayer of gratitude for the mountain that helped her follow through with her resolve to focus on what she would do, and to give her daughter the space to do the same.

§

Focusing on what you will do can bring balance and peace to your relationship with your children and is the basis of empowering both parent and child.

Notice that there are two points of power in our relationships. We can end power struggles and empower both our children and ourselves when:

1. We choose to perceive the behavior differently. Changing judgment to curiosity helps with this.
2. We choose to *act* rather than *react,* and we refuse to allow our child's behavior to press our buttons.

Don't discipline in anger

Taking care of our own emotions in the stressful times of childrearing is a momentous task. When kids are hard to handle, they are our greatest teachers in how to handle ourselves. Learn to recognize when your buttons are being pushed and do *not* attempt to discipline when you are emotionally charged and angry. Calm down first!

Screaming, yelling, and scolding are verbal assaults on another person. It draws enormous amounts of trust from our emotional bank account with that person. Having said that, also recognize that I don't know anyone who *hasn't* screamed or yelled at his or her children at some time in their life. So don't beat yourself up if this is a tactic you have been using to try to get your child to change. Just recognize that it is not effective, as it hurts the relationship and both of you as individuals. If you *do* find yourself screaming, apologize later. If you know you're about to blow, sending out a warning and yelling, "Run!" gives kids (and partners) a chance to clear out!

> Focusing on what **you** will do can bring balance and peace to your relationship with your children and is the basis of empowering both parent and child.

When you are calm, help your child to drain frustrations. You'll find some hands-on tools for doing this in the next chapter.

Next time your children press your buttons, remember that your power lies within you, behind your eyes. They can only press your buttons if you let them. As soon as you choose not to react, their behavior changes as well. Be aware that their behavior may at first intensify, and they may press harder. However, if you *stay focused calmly on what you will do,* your child will eventually claim his own power and decide what he will do in light of the new circumstances.

Thoughts to ponder about power

Have you ever noticed that the moment you try to *make* someone feel or do something, his or her immediate reaction is resistance? As soon as we feel pushed in any way, our first tendency is to push back.

Dr. Gordon Neufeld, one of my favorite parenting educators, illustrated this concept very well in the following scenario. Imagine yourself in the line at the grocery store. If someone comes up from behind and gives you a push, your first tendency is not likely to turn around and say, "Thank you very much, I was going that way anyway!" No, your first reaction is likely to become defensive and to dig in your heels. It is human nature.

It is no different when our children feel pushed. They will automatically push back. Typically, we feel that they are defying our authority, and we push harder. They become more entrenched in their resistance; it now becomes a matter of pride for our children *not* to change the behavior we were trying to change. Even if they *wanted* to before, they will *not* change it now. The child now has a position to defend.

For example, try telling your two-year-old (or your 13-year-old) that he should, or *must*, put on his coat. He says he doesn't need to. You insist. He resists again. Continued struggle and argument will only further entrench him in his own position. (Remember that we are much more likely to believe and act on what *we* are saying than on what we hear *others* saying!)

So how do we let go, and free and encourage children to make effective changes that work for both of us?

- *Look at the big picture; choose to create rather than to react.* In every interaction with your child, proactively look for the positive. Start searching for and commending your child's positive traits, actions, ideas, feelings, and talents. As you focus more on the positive, much of the negative will fade away naturally.

- *Recognize that if your child is struggling for power, she may be telling you she is ready for more power in her life.* Gradually stepping back and allowing children to have more power in their lives is one of the toughest challenges parents face. Yes, we needed to dress them completely when they were babies. If they needed to burp, that was our problem, too. As they grow, however, they want and need to learn to dress themselves, choose their own outfits, and gradually make more and more decisions on their own. This is their power.

- *Find alternatives to "no" and use them.*
  - ~ Your two-year-old comes hobbling toward you with a knife in his hand. Instead of saying "No, no!" and taking the knife away, take the knife away saying, "I've been looking for that! Thank you for bringing it to me!"
  - ~ "Can I have a cookie, Mom?" Instead of saying, "No, not now!" try saying, "Yes, right after dinner."

~ If your teen daughter approaches you with her new friends, all clad in leather and chains, and asks, "Dad, can I go to the mall?" don't just say "no." You know you'll have a battle on your hands and she'll find a way to go anyway. Be honest with her. Say, "I have some concerns about that. Convince me you'll be safe." See what she knows about taking care of herself. Too often, we simply launch into a lecture about safety, but never find out what she already knows. Asking her to convince you gives her credibility and will help you understand how prepared she is to take care of herself.

Give children choices, as they are ready for them. Teach them to make their own decisions about what they'd like to wear, eat, play, etc. As they exercise power in a positive manner, they'll have less need to gain it by pressing your buttons.

If we're worried about what others think, it can be difficult to let our kids choose their own clothing. Worrying about the image our kids project to the world can be the basis of many power struggles. I've learned to just get over it!

§

BETH CRINGED as her daughter Sara loped out the door, her vest on backwards and her rubber boots nearly touching her long shorts. Beth had listened to Barbara Coloroso talk about how important it is to let kids make their own decisions as long as "it isn't life threatening, unhealthy, or morally threatening." Ms. Coloroso had gone on to suggest that if parents are concerned about the reflection their child's dress might have on their own image, they can make up a little button for their child to wear stating, "I dressed myself!"

Beth never really thought that was necessary. After all, wasn't it obvious Sara dressed herself? Couldn't everyone tell that at a glance? One day, Beth came home from work and there was her 8-year-old daughter with a "pony tail" in her hair. The odd thing was the placement of it – it protruded from the top of her head like a unicorn's horn! "Oh, Sara," Beth said carefully, "Did you wear your hair like that to school today dear?"

"Uh-huh," came the jocular reply. "D'ya like it, Mom?"

"Oh, it certainly is different." Beth tried to match her daughter's cheerfulness while secretly praying that the other moms – the ones who could always be there to pick up their children after school – would realize that Sara had done her hair herself.

The hairdo and the incident fell silently away until one afternoon about three weeks later. Leaving work early, Beth arrived at the school to surprise her daughter.

"Hi, Mom!" Sara said excitedly. "Come on, I'll show you my portrait." Beth followed Sara to the back of the classroom. The back wall was filled with "shadow portraits" which captured each child's side profile in black mounted on bright orange construction paper. Someone had taken a lot of time to painstakingly draw every last detail.

Then she saw it! There, right in between the bulletin boards, in a row all its own, was a carefully drawn side portrait of a little girl's head – with a unicorn-like ponytail protruding in the front!

"I'll show you mine, Mom!" Sara's voice rang out cheerfully.

"Oh, it's all right dear," Beth tried to match her cheerfulness, "I think I just found it!"

Little more was said and the event was fading away until Beth met another mom when she was picking her daughter up from a birthday party.

"Oh!" exclaimed the other mom, "are you the one who did your daughter's hair for the portrait picture?"

"Oh no," Beth replied. "My daughter makes her own decisions about what she wears, and she can do her hair all by herself!" Beth was a little surprised that, rather than being embarrassed, she was inwardly glowing with the pride she felt in her daughter's independence.

§

It's interesting how, when we work to build our child's self-esteem, our own self-esteem improves as well!

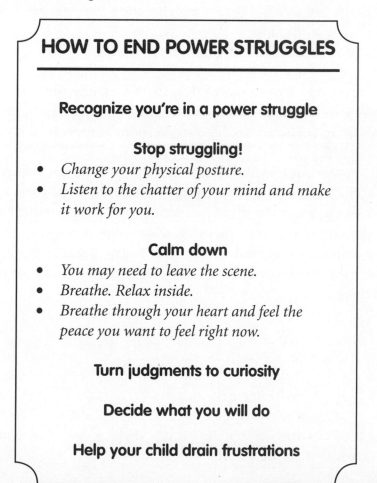

HOW TO END POWER STRUGGLES

Recognize you're in a power struggle

Stop struggling!
- *Change your physical posture.*
- *Listen to the chatter of your mind and make it work for you.*

Calm down
- *You may need to leave the scene.*
- *Breathe. Relax inside.*
- *Breathe through your heart and feel the peace you want to feel right now.*

Turn judgments to curiosity

Decide what you will do

Help your child drain frustrations

Summary

Building a strong and healthy relationship with your child is the best way to increase the self-esteem of both of you. When you claim your true power, your child learns to claim his. Remember that true power lies behind your eyes, in the gap between stimulus and response. Notice when you are in a power struggle, let go, and redirect your attention by focusing on what *you* will do, and by giving your child the space to decide what *she* will do.

Turn judgment to curiosity to open up your relationship with your child and to help her deal with her emotions. Understanding that emotions drive behavior and helping your child to release emotions is the key to helping her take "response-ability" in each situation. Deal with her feelings rather than simply treating her negative behavior with a negative reaction

Respect your child's boundaries and he will learn to respect yours.

If your child is always struggling for power, give him more! Find positive ways he can take more responsibility in his life and contribute to the family. Let him make his own decisions as soon as he is capable of doing so.

Be patient with yourself and realize that you cannot change years of conditioning and habits overnight. However, as you consciously practice perceiving the stimuli in your life in a more positive light, and drawing back and choosing your response, your circle of empowerment will continue to expand. Its expansion brings new joy, deeper appreciation, and greater depth to your life and to the lives of your children.

4

The Way of Emotional Grounding

Dealing with Feelings – Your's & Your Child's

Negative feelings expressed and accepted lose their destructive power.
– Dorothy Corkille Briggs

Feelings point toward underlying needs.

Emotions and our ability to deal with them are the determining factor in developing successful relationships with our children. Many of us have tremendous difficulty dealing with emotions – some of us don't even want to utter the word "emotion." That's because the traditional way of dealing with them has been to stuff them under the carpet and pretend they don't exist. "Oh no, I'm not angry. I've never been angry…" "There'll be none of *that (crying, yelling, misery)* in this house, young lady!" "Wipe those tears from your eyes or I'll give you something to cry about!" "Oh come on now, big boys don't cry!"

When many of us were children and were emotional and had a problem, *we* were the problem. Our emotions got us into trouble so we fought to stuff them down and seal them away – forever.

The problem is that emotions are energy in motion. In our struggle to shut down our emotions, they become trapped in our bodies and are the fundamental cause of stress and dis-ease.

To allow and even draw out our children's emotions is a tremendous leap from what traditional parenting has taught us to do. Dealing with emotions is way out of our comfort zone. However, just because it isn't in our comfort zone to deal with emotions isn't a reason not to deal with them. Emotions exist, they are real, and they will continue to create difficulties until we learn to deal with them.

Emotions are the key to connecting with others. If we want to connect with our kids we'll have to push our comfort zones. It may help us to do that if we recognize that our comfort zones may not be keeping us as comfortable as we think. What is our comfort zone but our known territory – the roles that we play in life, the old scripts that we utter again and again? Are these old scripts and this known territory keeping us comfortable, or are they making us *uncomfortable*?

Congratulate yourself as you break through confining comfort zones and begin to deal with emotions that allow you and your children to connect in deep and meaningful ways. Think of how much easier life will be for your children as they learn to deal with their emotions. Teaching them to deal with their emotions enables them to handle their own behavior, from the inside out.

We are in crisis today because we have not learned to deal with emotions. This is your dangerous opportunity to explore new territory and to discover the joy of truly connecting with your child.

Please see me! Hear me! Understand me!
– the power of listening

Who doesn't want to be heard, to be understood, to truly be listened to? Really listening and being present with your child is a powerful way to help your child deal with emotions and to deepen your relationship. Learning how to truly listen involves a whole lot more than simply developing a few skills. Empathetic listening means listening with our head and with our heart. It requires that we stay alert to our child's feelings and needs. The acronym ALERT helps us remember the components of empathetic listening.

A – ATTITUDE is vital! It's 90 percent of listening. Let go of emotions that interfere with your ability to hear your child. Set your own agenda aside. This means not jumping to inform, teach, or even guide him to a solution. Be prepared to hear him out, from the beginning to the end.

L – LISTEN soul-ly to understand. Lay aside all judgments and defensiveness. Just be curious. Every time a judgment or defensive reaction comes up, turn it to curiosity and remain open to listening. Let your child open up.

E – EMPATHIZE with your child. Put yourself in her shoes. *Feel what she feels, while staying very clear that these are her feelings, not yours.* You don't need to fix her emotions, just hear and acknowledge them. Adopt a similar body language to hers. Reflecting her body language shows you're listening and can give you important information about what she's feeling. Don't mimic every move, of course. However, if she is slumped over and leaning on the table, you'll understand her better and she'll be more willing to open up if you sit beside her and slump over. Buzzing about like Madame Butterfly, or sitting or standing in a confrontational manner, can shut down all communication.

R – REFLECT back to your child what you understand him to be saying and feeling. Summarize and rephrase the content. Give the feeling a name. Guessing is fine. He will correct you if you're wrong.

T – TURN the floor over to them! You can't listen if you're the one talking, so be quiet and listen! Give them time to speak. Most people wait less than two seconds before they talk again. Give your child time to gather his thoughts. Count how long you wait for answers. Try counting to at least seven before you say anything and notice any improvement in your relationship with your child and in his ability to express himself.

Tips for making empathetic listening work

Here are some sentence stems and examples of how to reflect feelings.

- *Sounds like* you are pretty disappointed that you didn't get an invitation to Cheri's party.
- Shoelaces are really hard to do up. *I can see how* frustrated you are.
- Having a younger brother follow you around everywhere *can feel annoying.*
- *Could it be that* you were a little embarrassed when you couldn't answer the question your teacher asked you?
- *I can see how* excited you are about your Christmas party!
- *I sense* maybe you felt a little shy around the new student.
- *Correct me if I'm wrong,* but it sounds like you're a little jealous of your friend.
- *I get the impression that* you're feeling a little nervous about your swimming trip.
- *Sounds to me like* you're pretty pleased with yourself!
- *So you're feeling* kind of depressed about your math homework.
- *It seems as though* you're overwhelmed with all of this homework.
- *I hear you saying* you'd like to send your baby sister back to the hospital. It's hard to share Mommy's/Daddy's attention with a new baby.
- *Could it be that* you'd like to spend a little more time just with you and me?
- *I hear you!* It's *not* easy sitting through class listening to a boring teacher.
- *I wonder if* you are a little tired after your long day.
- *Is it possible that you're feeling…*
- *Let me see if I'm with you…*

Guessing is much better than simply asking your child how she feels or why she's done something for two reasons.

1. She may not be able to give her feelings a name.
2. "Why" questions are often received as an interrogation and quickly shut down communication. Even if not interpreted as an

interrogation, we often *don't* know "why," and so it shuts us down again.

Get beneath the anger

Anger is a secondary emotion. Some other emotion(s) triggered the anger. But usually the anger is all we see. It is when we get to the emotion beneath the anger that real release, understanding, and healing begin. For example, once you've acknowledged your child's anger at being left behind the day of his field trip, help him explore the emotion underneath the anger. You might say, "Sounds like you were really *disappointed* about not going on the trip." Then give him a chance to respond. He may just be grateful that someone understands, or he may correct you. Either way, you've helped him clarify his emotion. This shows him you're really listening and trying to understand him. That's powerfully helpful in clearing the anger and the emotions underneath. Discovering the underlying emotions will also be helpful in identifying unmet needs.

> Think back to the last time you were angry. What set it off? Were you disappointed, frustrated, hurt? Many emotions can set off the anger. These emotions underneath the anger are the ones you want to identify and communicate. So look for those emotions with your children. When you've identified the underlying emotions, they will feel understood.

Sometimes children prefer to show you how they feel

The Emotions Chart at the back of this book (see page 235) is a marvelous tool to help both you and your child become aware of, identify, and give emotions a name. The importance of *emotional intelligence* today cannot be overstated. I kept the Emotions Chart on my fridge for years to help me identify my own emotions, and to help my children identify theirs. For younger children, try selecting six to ten emotions to start with and put them where they can readily be seen. Older children love to draw these faces for younger children. Encourage the younger children to draw the faces too. Select some enjoyable emotions along with the uncomfortable ones. Have your child identify how he's feeling at various times in the day.

Avoid the urge to solve or fix the problem for your child

Simply releasing the feeling is all that is necessary. If the child asks for advice or help, imagine yourself alongside your child and set the problem or issue of concern in front of both of you. Work together to generate possible solutions (more on this in the next chapter). *Allow your child to own the problem. Be their support.* If your child does not have the skills to handle the problem, help him to gain those skills.

Empathetic listening is powerful. It is a very intimate act for it allows you to "in to me see." Intimacy is the result of listening empathically without judgment. Feeling truly understood helps to fulfill the great human need to belong.

Listening so your child feels heard and understood reduces discipline hassles and improves the quality of your relationship.

Temper tantrums – theirs and yours!

Anyone who has ever lived with a screamer knows that the fear of an impending temper tantrum can dominate family life. When I was learning the principles behind dealing with emotions, I understood that it was good for children to express their feelings – and if that meant crying, well, okay… but did they have to *wail?* I couldn't stand wailing. And underneath it all, I felt I was a failure as a parent if my child cried too much. I wanted to hear people say, "Isn't he a good baby. He's so quiet. He just smiles and smiles." I took pride in those comments, and I didn't want anyone to really know he cried. I felt as if I had done something wrong if he wasn't "good tempered."

Then along came my screamer – and there was no hiding or disguising her crying! When she screamed, it hurt everyone's ears and got on everyone's nerves. So naturally, we *all* wanted to avoid it. We started to tiptoe around, being careful not to set her off. The tiptoeing became a way of life, and still, the screaming didn't stop. In fact, I think the tension grew worse. Often it is this very tiptoeing, this walking on eggshells, that actually prevents the screamer from releasing her tension. Have you ever noticed how calm a child becomes after a screaming episode?

§

SHORTLY AFTER TERRY brought her second son home from the hospital, she noticed her oldest son, Nathan, was out of sorts. He'd been cranky and owlish all morning, and as Terry was about to sit down and nurse his brother, Nathan threw himself on the floor and started beating his feet against the chair, and screaming and wailing at the top of his lungs. Terry was about to yell at him to stop (as if that would have done any good!), when suddenly she felt a flash of what he was going through. This was tough going, sharing Mom's attention with a new baby brother, and such intimate attention at that!

Terry realized that Nathan's feelings were spilling over and he needed to feel loved and cared for *right now*. So she put his baby brother in his lounge chair and walked over and picked up her eldest. Nathan protested at first, but Terry held him tight and murmured, "It really has been difficult for you, sharing your mom with your baby brother. It's probably hard to see him getting all that attention and love." The screaming turned to deep sobbing as Nathan lay his head on Terry's shoulder and melted against her.

Terry let go of any idea that she was a "bad" mom because he was crying and carrying on. Instead, she felt grateful that he could let go and that she could help him drain his frustrations. "Oh, honey, maybe we haven't had enough time together just you and I. You know I love you just as much as I always did, and even more, because now with your brother here I have even more love in my heart, and you get it, too." Nathan calmed right down and Terry felt the tension that had been building for days leave his little body. She realized that she had been avoiding "setting him off" and that not meeting his emotions head-on had contributed to the stress and tension everyone felt. Suddenly, Nathan said, "Mommy, I think Caleb is hungry now!" and scooted off to play with his dump truck. Terry marveled at the peacefulness that seemed to settle over the entire household once Nathan's frustration had been recognized, allowed, and drained.

$§$

Dealing with temper tantrums means remembering it is okay for your child to drain his or her frustrations.

When I finally learned to stay calm even in the midst of my daughter's temper tantrums, they grew fewer and further between. We stopped trying to avoid the tantrums and met them head-on. I would hold my frustrated and out-of-control daughter on my knee, while I told myself over and over that I was helping her drain her frustrations in a healthy way. I reassured myself that I was not a "bad" mom because she screamed and cried. I learned to breathe deeply, to relax, and to let go of my own resistance to the screaming. I learned to go to the center of peace within me, and to stay there regardless of the chaos around me. "The only state I need to manage is my own," I'd tell myself. "Stop resisting what *is* and insisting on what *isn't*."

In his fabulous book *The Power of Now*, Eckhart Tolle says there really are only two inner states: either we are resisting, or we are not. It is *our resistance* to what *is* that causes us pain. To let go of resistance, which is the source of our anxiety, we must be willing to *surrender* to what is right now, rather than to insist on what isn't.

Of course, occasionally the screaming would get to me, and, if I felt I was going to "lose it," I'd head for the bathroom and lock myself in. She'd follow along and lay down outside the door, still kicking and screaming. I'd spend my time focusing on calming down. Sometimes I'd even have a shower. I always knew she was all right because I could still hear the kicking and screaming above the noise of the shower. When I was prepared to deal with her, I'd emerge.

Today, I thank my daughter tremendously for the gift of learning to stay centered and calm in the midst of chaos and turmoil. It is one of the many significant life lessons she taught me.

Remember that it is not up to you to *make* your child stop screaming. This is your opportunity to teach yourself to stay calm and to help her drain her frustrations. Focus on what *you* will do.

In a parenting group, as we were working with this concept, one mom shared the following story.

§

WE WERE SHOPPING and sure enough my child threw the classic temper tantrum right there in the middle of the department store. I thought about what you said, about what I could do. The only thing I could think of doing was what I *felt* like doing. So I got down on the floor beside him and started pounding the floor with my fists, kicking and screaming alongside him! My son stopped his temper tantrum immediately and sat up very concerned. "Mommy," he shook my shoulder, "Mommy, what are you doing? Stop, Mommy, stop!"

§

Well, that's one way to end a temper tantrum!

Years ago, I went to hear Dr. Gordon Neufeld speak. He specializes in helping children deal with hostile and aggressive emotions. At the break, I asked him to sum up what advice I could take back and give to the parents of children with Attention Deficit Disorder. He said, *"Teach kids to drain frustrations, and help them to make attachments."*

The root of violence is frustration, and frustration is a result of our attachments not working in our life. When our relationships with others aren't working, we become frustrated because we have an attachment to those people. So when a child is frustrated because his attachment with us is not working, and we send that child into isolation, away from us, we actually increase the frustration.

Dr. Neufeld stresses that it is important to be present to help and to witness our child draining frustration. He emphasizes the importance of a child "hitting the wall of futility" and encourages parents to help their child dissolve frustration with tears. He suggests urging a child who is close to tears to cry, by saying something like, "Oh it is so disappointing when things don't work out" in a teary kind of voice.

Emotions that are not released in a healthy way go underground and come out in behavior. If we use fear to temporarily shut down emotions, our child will become more frustrated and his behavior will become more violent. Oh, he may not dare to act out as long as the threatening adult is right in front of him, but his behavior will become more violent and out-of-control when the immediate threat is removed. This explains why some parents believe that very strict discipline and punishment "works." "He never acts like that around me," says the parent who uses fear to control his child, while the other parent finds herself dealing with emotional outbreak after emotional outbreak. She may find herself questioning her own parenting. Some parents have even told me that they feel their child is "allergic" to them, because he only cries around them. Allowing and encouraging children to cry and to release frustration is not wrong. On the contrary, these parents can congratulate themselves that they provide a safe space for their child to do so.

Children need a safe space to release emotions or they will keep them bottled up until they explode. At my first parent-teacher interview with my daughter's kindergarten teacher, the teacher asked me if Arleigh ever showed any emotion! Arleigh? Was she joking? Did she have her confused with someone else? Emotion was *all* we got at home, *especially* since she started school. In fact, temper tantrums that had finally been settling down escalated tenfold in those first few months of school.

"Oh! I get it now!" I thought, "At school, Arleigh had sealed her emotions away completely, banking them and storing them until she got home. No wonder we were going through a temper tantrum revival!" Arleigh continued to save her bottled-up emotions and frustration for us, until she could trust herself to express her emotions safely at school. It took time, years actually, but today she is very emotionally aware and understands how to deal with her sensitive nervous system.

Feelings point to needs

Sometimes, simply identifying feelings or emotions isn't enough. Sometimes we've expressed the feeling, but it's still there... "Okay, yes, I know I'm angry, I feel the anger...but what can I do about it?" Feelings point to needs. Once I've identified that I'm angry, I may still need to physically release the anger. Maybe I'm angry because someone has crossed my boundaries. I may need to clarify my boundaries with that person. The child who had the temper tantrum in the store may have a need for sleep, or a need for some quiet time with his parent, or a need to run, jump, tumble, and play.

Recently, in a parenting class, we were discussing the needs indicated by various emotions. We drew up a chart that looked something like this:

Feeling	Need
Sad	Compassion, permission/ encouragement to cry; hug; space to be alone
Cranky	Sleep; exercise; attention
Depressed	Expression; love; understanding; inspiration

You can see that it is not always easy to determine the need. Making the connection between feeling and the need is the challenge of parenting. Please know that, often, the need is simply to be understood and we can fulfill that need by listening. Take note the next time you give your child your full attention and listen so that she knows she has been heard and understood. Very often there won't be any problem left to solve! Having expressed her feelings, she'll scoot off to play, the entire episode forgotten.

However, sometimes uncomfortable feelings and behavior persist, even after the child has been heard. Stay alert to the underlying need that the feeling is pointing to and encourage your child to take action to meet that need. It is not your responsibility to solve your child's problems or to make her happy. However you *can* help her connect the feeling to the need and help *her* find ways to meet her needs.

Some needs take time to meet. It took time, patience, and persistence for Arleigh to learn to identify and express her feelings, but the growth and lessons learned have been well worth it.

Tools to help kids release frustration

- *Encourage and witness the physical release of emotions.* If your child wants to throw things in her anger, give her something she can throw. If she wants to hit, give her something to punch.

  Sometimes simply being there to witness her emotional pain is enough. Karen had a child with special needs who repeatedly came home from school upset and frustrated. He would throw himself against the wall and slowly slide down it until he was sitting on the floor. Karen discovered that simply being there to witness her son's agony helped a lot. She'd sit down beside him, he'd cry it out, and then away he'd go.

  Aletha Solter, in her book *Tears and Tantrums*, recommends holding young children on your knee, stroking their forehead, looking into their eyes, and soothing them by assuring them it's all right to cry, etc. Tears are an excellent way to release stress, and children have lots of stress too. Tell yourself, "I'm helping her to release stress and drain frustrations."

- *Stop trying to "fix" your child and her problems and simply be there to listen to her first.* Sometimes we create problems and shut down emotions because we believe we have to fix those emotions.
- *Use empathetic listening to identify emotions.*
- *Identify unmet needs.* Once your child knows you've heard her, you can then look for the underlying needs the emotions reveal. Often her needs are met by being heard. However, if her needs have not yet been met, help her discover how to meet them.
- *Give young children their wishes in fantasy.* "I know it's hard when you want Cheerios really, really badly, and there are none. I wish we had some, too. In fact, I wish we had a great big giant-sized box bigger than this whole kitchen." Young children often feel really understood when we give them their wishes in fantasy.

Do not give in to children's temper tantrum demands just to "keep the peace." You will find the price of peace gets higher and higher as children become more demanding. However, do not make the emotion they are releasing wrong. If your child throws herself on the floor of the grocery store because you won't buy her candy, focus on what *you* will do – perhaps calmly picking her up and carrying her out (or throwing yourself down beside her!). Do not give her the candy just to keep her quiet or she learns to use her temper tantrums as a ploy. She may, however, feel so frustrated and desperate to get the candy that she is indeed out of control. Stay calm and honor the release of her emotions, but do not give in to her demands!

Recognize when it's a real temper tantrum and the child is genuinely out of control, and when it's an "I'm going to scream and holler 'cause I know that gets me what I want" temper tantrum. If you decide to leave the room and the "temper tantrum" gets up relatively calmly and follows you, then begins again, beware! It may be nothing more than a manipulative tactic, and you don't want to give that too much attention. In such cases, check out how *you* feel. If you are merely annoyed, it is probably a ploy for attention. Ignoring it or providing a distraction for your child may be your best bet in that case.

Helping Defensive Children Unlock Emotion

"But how do I deal with children who lock their feelings away and who are very defensive? What if my child doesn't *want* to talk about what's bugging him?" Dr. Neufeld suggests touching those feelings lightly – as if you're touching a bruise. Say something like, "That must have been very disappointing for you," and then get out of there. Don't wait around for the child to argue or push you away, but let them know that you're empathizing with them and that you are there if they want to talk.

When dealing with young children's emotions remember that when they *have* an emotion, they *are* the emotion. For this reason, Dr. Neufeld refers to three- to five-year-olds as the most aggressive people on the face of the planet! They know they shouldn't hit, but their frustration takes over and by the time they remember they're not supposed to, they've already hit. Parents who understand this will be able to help their young children drain their emotional frustration and aid their child in growing into emotional awareness and control.

Practice releasing tension & stress on a regular basis

Here are some more ideas to help you and your children release tension and drain frustrations. Practice the ones that appeal to you when frustration hits or when you start to feel it building. *Practice on a regular basis.* Many parents' lives have changed when they have included routine times for the kids to swim, run, climb, or just "hang out."

- Dance, bike, jog, swim, etc.
- Do an anger dance.
- Take time to ask yourself what you want and /or need.
- Rip up old newspapers or magazines and throw them about.
- Stomp out of the house and walk briskly until your anger dissipates.
- Stop what you're doing and get everyone out to the park.
- Punch a beanbag chair, or pillow.
- Install a punching bag and go at it regularly.

- Take a towel and beat on the bathtub with it.
- Beat your small rugs outside.
- Say, "I'm going to scream for…number of minutes." Then do it. Make angry sounds, but eliminate words that might hurt others.
- Go outside and throw a basketball against the house.
- Throw dirty laundry around. (If you throw clean laundry, you'll have to fold it later!)
- Scream, "Run!" and clear house.
- Throw soft toys, Nerf balls, or anything else that won't damage things.
- Whip marshmallows into the sink and yell a karate-type yell as you throw. (Caution: *Fresh* marshmallows are less likely to ricochet!)
- Take a shower or a bath to calm down. Let the water wash the negative feelings away.
- Pile up pillows or inflated inner tubes and smash them with a tennis racket using your whole body. Keep knees bent.
- Take at least half an hour for yourself every day, without outside stimuli.
- Turn off the TV.
- Add your own…

Some children respond well to an "angry blanket" that they can throw on the floor and stand on to scream and holler. One parent told me they had two anger blankets in their home – one for her daughter and one for her, and often they were both in use at the same time!

Auditory people may prefer to record their feelings, share them with others, or to listen to soothing music.

Visual people may prefer to imagine tense, frustrated emotions draining out of them. It may help them to visualize calm, peaceful surroundings.

Kinesthetic people (and most children fall into this category) may prefer to blow out their emotions – Karate yells and chops, anger dances, throwing soft toys or laundry, punching a pillow or punching bag, and shaking and wiggling out emotions can be helpful for these people.

Being proactive and helping children drain frustrations on a regular basis can save everyone a lot of anguish.

§

IN GRADE 4, KENNY was the discipline problem in a kindergarten-to-grade-12 school. He was in a fight at least once a day, and often five or six times a day. His teacher, Jayme, was a wreck trying to protect the other children. She recognized that Kenny had a lot of frustrations and that the way he liked to express frustration was through punching. So she decided to get him something he could punch. After meeting with the principal and the resource teacher, she bought gloves and a punching bag, and secured the bag to the wall outside the resource room. She told Kenny, "I can see how angry you get and how you want to punch when you get angry. Next time you want to punch something, I want you to stop and go directly to the punching bag and punch it. You don't have to ask, just go!"

Kenny asked if he could punch that bag when he got there in the morning. (He was always early.) "Certainly," replied Jayme. "Provided the school is open, of course," she added in a half-joking manner, not too certain what Kenny might do to get to the punching bag.

Kenny arrived at school bright and early the next morning and went directly to the punching bag. Jayme watched him out of the corner of her eye as he worked up a major sweat. After half an hour, he finally quit. That morning he settled right down in class. In fact, it didn't take long until he practically quit hitting other kids completely. Kenny went from five or six fights a day, to one or two in the last eight months of school that year. The opportunity to drain his frustrations safely made all the difference in the world to Kenny, not to mention the difference it made to Jayme and the rest of the class.

§

The place to learn how to calm down and smooth out your thoughts and emotions is not in the heat of the moment. You wouldn't ask someone to run a marathon without practicing and training on a regular basis, would you? Then why would you expect yourself to be able to handle marathon emotions without regular training?

Take time periodically during the day, and especially before bed to focus your attention inward and notice whether you are relaxed. If you practice noticing tension and releasing it, you'll be ready when your emotions are put to the test.

Dealing with Anger and Aggression

The key to helping children deal with aggression and anger is to remain calm and look past the behavior to the underlying feelings that generate the behavior.

Allow appropriate and safe release of the anger, and use empathic listening to acknowledge and release underlying emotions.

Help children understand that they are not their feelings. They are not "bad" because they have "bad" feelings.

Feelings are separate from behavior.
All feelings are okay.

Aggressive and hostile behavior towards others is not okay.

Teach your child to release anger and to do what they can do about the situation, focusing on their true power, "What will I do?"

Putting It all together

The following story illustrates the principles of empathetic listening and the Circle of Empowerment in action.

§

I WAS BUSY GETTING READY to facilitate a parenting class and didn't pay much attention to my nine-year-old son when he came home from school. I didn't really notice what was going on with him, although I did sense that something was not quite right. However, he wasn't complaining – loudly, that is – and since there were no major episodes to intervene in, no fights to settle, and no quarrels to resolve, I kept working feverishly. All went well until the phone rang.

It was a business call. Would I facilitate a parenting course? I was just about to respond affirmatively when my son came around the corner, took one look at me with the phone glued to my ear, and broke out into a full-fledged temper tantrum:

"AHHHHHHH!!!! YOU'RE ALWAYS ON THE PHO-O-O-O-O-N-E! AHHHH!!"

Horrified, I took a deep breath, said a hurried, "Just a minute please," into the phone, covered the receiver, and whispered fiercely, "Jason, get downstairs – NOW!"

My words must have carried enough urgency to move him in spite of his anger, for he reluctantly took himself and his temper tantrum down the stairs to his room.

Struggling to regain composure, I pulled myself together, calmed my voice, and returned to my caller. "Certainly I'll do that class for you," I said smoothly, and then added by way of explanation, "Just a minor temper tantrum with one of the younger children. You know how it is." I laughed weakly to lighten it up a bit and got off the phone as soon as possible.

The moment the receiver hit the cradle, however, I headed down the stairs to give that son of mine a piece of my mind. "Oh-h-h," I muttered to myself, "Just *wait* 'til I get to him. How *dare* he come screaming around the corner like that when I'm on the phone? How would he like it if I weren't even here when he got home? If I can't run a business from home, I'll have to go out and get a job! How am I supposed to run a business from home when he acts like that?"

On and on my self-righteous chatter continued, until somewhere, from the deep recesses of my mind a still small voice said, "Maggie, don't you think you ought to practice what you preach? What happened to dealing with the feelings that drive the behavior? You know how you tell everyone to open up the relationship and find out the emotion that's driving the behavior? Whatever happened to turning judgment to curiosity? "

"Oh yeah," I muttered back to myself, "Okay, turn judgment into curiosity." And as soon as that thought entered my mind, my anger began to dissipate. What *was* bugging him anyway? Why would he explode like that? Suddenly my driving need was to find out what had happened to Jason and to help him release the emotions that had caused the outburst. "Calm down," I reminded myself. "Never discipline when angry."

By the time I knocked on Jason's door, I was completely calm and openly curious. "Jason," I asked softly, "Can I come in?"

"Ummhum!" came the gruff and sullen reply.

I took that to mean yes, and pushed the door open to see Jason sitting on the edge of the bed, his chin in one hand, glaring at the floor in front of him. To really get on side with him and understand where he was coming from, I copied his body language. Walking over quietly, I turned and sat down on the bed beside him, put my chin in both my hands, and stared at the same spot he was focused on.

"Wow," I said quietly, "I haven't seen you that angry in along time!"

"Yeah, well you're *always* on the *phone*," came the abrupt and irritated reply.

"Whoa, it *really* bothered you to come around the corner and see me on the phone." I did my best to just listen and encourage him to continue.

"It's like your *business* is more important than *we* are!" Jason spat the words out vehemently. I felt like I'd been kicked in the stomach, and my first impulse was to defend my position and assure him that he was of course more important than my business. But remembering why I was there, I told myself, "Stay curious – get to the root of the emotion." So instead, I said, "I guess you *really* wanted to talk to me right then…"

"Hmmm," Jason grunted again.

I still wasn't sure what was going on, but I figured something must have happened at school, so I just guessed out loud: "Something must have happened at school."

Bingo! I knew I'd hit the hot button, because as soon as I said that, Jason burst into tears. I watched incredulously as a flood of emotions rocked his body and came gushing out. Jason told me falteringly about how one of his friends at school had humiliated him right in the middle of the gym floor at lunch hour. He had been carrying these pent up feelings since then.

"Whoa," I thought, "I nearly sealed that off with my intended lecture." I was glad I was taking the time to listen and to help him release those emotions now. Just imagine how much time I would have spent dealing with those emotions erupting later: the squabbling with siblings, hostile feelings between Jason and me, being called to the school to deal with the aftermath of fights with the boy who'd humiliated him. I could see how those powerful emotions had to be released somehow.

I listened and empathized with Jason. "No wonder you're so upset. That's a tough situation to handle. Sounds like you were really embarrassed."

"Yeah," Jason sighed, grateful that someone finally understood.

Just then his father came home. "What's going on?" asked his dad.

Again, Jason repeated the whole story, this time far more coherently than the first time.

His dad listened quietly and then said simply, "You know what I used to do when someone did something like that to me?"

"What?" asked a wide-eyed Jason.

"I used to draw *pictures* of what I'd like to do to him!"

Jason lit up immediately. Cartooning had been one of his favorite pastimes lately and it didn't take him long before he had pen in hand, drawing feverishly. I marveled at how much emotion he had around this issue, and watched him regain his sense of power with each new cartoon.

The first cartoons started out with Jason and "Bibi" (his tormentor) about the same size. But as the series continued, Jason began to get larger and larger, more and more powerful, until "Bibi" was the size of a mere mosquito on the paper.

Now, part of me was concerned about him drawing such violent pictures. But I reminded myself, "Emotions that are not released safely go underground and come out in behavior." Was this not a safe release of emotions? After all, no one was getting hurt and shortly thereafter Jason re-established his friendship with "Bibi"!

Handling the situation this way also helped to establish a strong and caring relationship between Jason and me. And after Jason had released his emotions, we sat down together to discuss the "phone incident."

"You know, Jason, I was embarrassed today, too. I was on a business call when you started screaming. You're not usually the one I worry about having a tantrum. So far I've been able to count on your help when I get on the phone."

"I know, Mom, I'm sorry." Jason really looked sorry.

"Well I don't want it to happen again."

"It won't, Mom."

"And that's not because my business is more important than you are.

"I know, Mom, I just said that." Jason looked a little sheepish.

"So can I count on you to help me keep the peace when the phone rings?"

"What do you mean?"

"Well, if I'm on the phone and your sister gets upset, do you think you could distract her?"

"Sure, Mom," Jason gave me a reassuring look. "Can I go now?"

I just smiled and off he went.

I smiled to myself again as I was tucking Jason into bed that night. I certainly didn't always do the right thing with this job of parenting, but tonight I could rest easy. Jason gave me an extra long hug.

"I love you, honey," I whispered.

"Love you too, Mom," Jason answered, and then, just as I was about to close the door, Jason said, "And, Mom – thanks."

Summary

Helping children learn to effectively handle their emotions is crucial to their health, and to the health of your relationship with them. Central to helping them, is your ability to handle your own emotions and control your inner environment. Teach yourself to stay centered and calm in the midst of your child's emotional turmoil and create a safe space for him to drain his frustrations. Teach him how to be aware of and to identify his emotions. Find and practice ways to drain your own frustrations. Discover and practice ways to pro-actively release stress, for you and your child. Make sure you both have time and space to let loose and "play."

Remember the acronym ALERT to help you employ principles of effective listening:
≠# Keep an open and accepting *attitude*
- *Listen* intently
- *Empathize* with your child.
- *Reflect* content and emotions back to your child.
- *Turn* the floor over to them and let them speak!

Only discipline and deal with your child when you are in charge of your *own* emotions.

5

The Way of Communication

Developing Meaningful Connections

Kids are people first!

Attitude is more important than the past, than education, than money, than circumstances, than failures, than successes, than what other people think or say or do.
— CHARLES SWINDOL

The secret of change is to focus all your energy, not on fighting the old, but on building the new.
— DAN MILMAN

No problem can be solved at the level at which it was created.
— ALBERT EINSTEIN

Think about the following conversation.
   "Honey, did you remember to take out the trash?"
   "Hmmm…"
"What's that, dear?"
"Hmmm…"
"Would that hmmm mean yes or no?"

"Hmmm…"

"Let's try it this way, "How about one 'hmmm' for yes and two 'hmmms' for no?"

Not an unusual conversation for many parents of teenagers. Now consider this conversation.

"Daddy, daddy, see what I got? See what I got?"

"Ummm-hmm," came the reply from underneath the hood of the car.

"Whatcha doin', Daddy?"

"Hmmm…"

"Daddy? Can I help, Daddy?"

"Hmmm… not now son…"

"What's that, Daddy, what's that? Daddy? See my picture, Daddy?"

"Um hmmm…"

Notice any similarities in the conversations? Such "conversations" may occur occasionally, but if they become the norm around your home, look out!

Teaching kids to speak, listen, & cooperate

How much time do you spend actually dialoguing with your child? A dialogue is like a game of ping pong; it's no fun unless you get to hit the ball back and forth. When was the last time you carried on a meaningful conversation with your child?

Yes, such conversations are possible at every age, although a meaningful conversation with a 2-year-old will obviously be different from a meaningful conversation with a 16-year-old. What they share in common is an interest in one another's lives, an open curiosity to know more, to share more. Let your curiosity open the door to communicating with your child. Who is she? What does she really like to do? How does she handle problems in her life? From a very early age, follow your child's lead. Keep simple toys that stimulate her imagination within her grasp. Instead of organizing her activities, step back and observe. Then join her in her play.

Ask open-ended questions such as "What would happen if…" or "What do you think…" Open-ended questions are questions that cannot be answered with yes or no. "Can you/do you/ will you/won't you/ are you/aren't you" are all closed response questions. What, how, when, where, and why are open-ended questions.

Send messages carefully and make sure they are received. Remember the ping pong game. How many times do we just hit the ball in our child's direction and hope they get it? Check to see that the ball was received and give her time to send it back! Most people ask a question and wait less than a second before they speak again. Try counting to seven after you've asked a question and notice how dialogue improves. Listen to your child's answer. We teach kids how to listen to us by showing them how we listen to them.

The best way to stay involved and connected to children is to appreciate them each step of the way. Do you remember when they were young and you could spend an entire evening just marveling at how they were learning? "Oh, look at that, he's pulling himself up on the sofa," Or, "I think he's getting ready to take his first step!" And when he took his first step and then fell because of his unsteady feet, did you reprimand him for not getting it right? Of course not! You understood that these "mistakes" were just part of the learning process.

Now take that attitude and apply it to their entire life, understanding that they need to go through a learning process in developing attitudes as well. Listen more to them as they grow into their teen years and appreciate the emotional, mental, spiritual, and physical stages of growth. Let go of lecturing, correcting, and instructing them each step of the way. Allowing and encouraging children to express their opinion is crucial to meaningful communication. Perhaps you can't accept their opinion at some point. That's okay. Just try allowing it. Stay open and curious and hear them, then express your opinion without lecturing.

Communicating openly and freely is the key to developing cooperation and effectively resolving conflicts. Make it a habit at all stages of your child's life. If until now you've been sending one-way messages, start today to apply the principles mentioned above. You'll be surprised how quickly communication will improve.

Do be careful, however, not to follow teenagers around bombarding them with questions! Teenagers, especially, need space. Refrain from instructing and lecturing, and be open and ready to receive.

Avoid using "why" if your child becomes defensive. Some kids have heard, "Now *why* would you do a thing like that?" spoken in an accusatory tone and automatically become defensive as soon as they hear the word. Reframe "why" questions by starting your question with "what," "how," "when," and "where."

Kids are people first!

Kids are people first! The key to meaningful communication is to speak with your child *person to person*, rather than parent to child. Many parents, however, have fallen into communication patterns with their children that diminish their children and damage their relationship.

When speaking with younger children, you may need to simplify your language, but keep your tone respectful and refrain from using baby talk. The latest brain research identifies the richness of the language in the home as one of the prime indicators of children's health and potential. They have measured the variety of words, the number of questions, the amount of dialogue, how many statements are made in a given time period, and so on. Results show a substantial difference in the child's vocabulary. By 26 months, children who came from a "vocabulary rich" environment had an average of 800 words. Children at the other end of the scale had average vocabularies of only 100 words at 26 months old.

To create a vocabulary-rich environment, talk with your children often and avoid speaking down to them. Baby talk may be cute, but it doesn't provide the learning environment children need to develop their vocabulary. Talking baby talk can become a habit that creates problems for your child.

§

SHERRY WAS VISITING with her friend Marti. Marti was getting ready to take her five-year-old to the speech pathologist. "I just don't understand why he's having so much trouble speaking," Marti said.

Just then her son appeared in the doorway. Marti turned to him, took one look at his unhappy face, and said, "Evvy (his name was Devon), 'on't 'ou wan' 'oo go 'oo 'own?"

Sherry looked at her friend in amazement, "Marti, do you always speak to him like that?"

"Like what?" Marti looked perplexed.

"In that kind of baby talk," replied Sherry.

"Baby talk?" Marti looked momentarily confused, and then a huge grin spread across her face as the "ah-ha!" set in. "Hey! Maybe that's why Devon's having trouble with his speech!"

"Well," Sherry offered hesitantly, "he *does* do a pretty good imitation of your "baby talk"!

§

Young children are usually wide open to sharing their ideas and thoughts, and are eager to learn about *you*. Chat with them like you would a friend. Tell them a bit about your day; share your opinions and listen to theirs. Even if they can't answer back yet, keep talking to them. Set babies up where they can see you working and talk to them.

It may appear that an older child does not want to share his thoughts or talk about his day. That's okay. Share *your* thoughts and talk about your day. Keep it light and non-judgmental. Remember, you are talking with a friend.

At a seminar I gave on communicating with children, a woman shared the following story with me.

§

ONE DAY as I was bustling about doing my housework, the doorbell rang. You can imagine my surprise when I opened the front door to see my four-year-old son standing there. "Jonathon, get in here!" I said automatically.

But Jonathon acted like he hadn't heard me and said, "Hello, Ruth! How are you? I've come for tea."

"Jonathon," I started to protest and he interrupted me again. "I've come for tea, Ruth," he repeated insistently. Suddenly, it was like I was hit with a lightning bolt and I understood what he was up to. He just wanted to be treated like one of my friends and this was his way of telling me that. So I changed my tune and invited him in respectfully. The two of us went up to the kitchen, poured ourselves some tea (although I do believe he opted for hot chocolate) and had a short little chat – person to person, friend to friend. The chat didn't take very long, but the lesson he taught me has lasted a lifetime. That was nearly 15 years ago, and even today we are more than mother and son – we're good friends, too.

§

Sometimes we get trapped in the roles we play: I'm the parent and you're the child; I'm supposed to…and you're supposed to. If we talked to our friends the way we talk to our children, how many friends would we have? We can get so caught up in our roles we never get to know the person behind the role. Often, it is these very roles that keep us separate from others. Leaving these roles often requires that we, once again, stretch out of our comfort zone.

Play is the connecting fiber in relationships

"Turning on De-Light Playshops" are workshops I offer that use storytelling, art, and dance to help people expand their comfort zone and to set their roles and masks aside. Recently, two sets of mom-and-daughter teams attended. We had a 17-year-old teenager and her mother, and a 75-year-old mother and her daughter. Each of the four broke through her comfort zone to participate in the activities. When they left their comfort zone, their "roles" fell away. They were no longer mother and daughter, each guarding her own place, but individuals experiencing and enjoying new aspects of themselves. Suddenly, they found themselves in the "connecting zone." They all experienced a new-found connection. The teenager and her mother claimed the experience a "miraculous breakthrough" in their relationship.

As we leave our comfort zone, we drop the roles we've clung to. It takes courage to push through that comfort zone because the walls of our zone are made of fear. When we hedge up against that fear and back down into our comfort zone, we give fear the power to reign. If, however, we feel the fear of challenging our comfort zone and move through it anyway, we move into a new zone. We discover new depths within ourselves. When we leave our comfort zone, we can enter the connecting zone. Subconsciously we send a message to our child, "Here I am, just me, getting to know a new dimension of me and connecting with an aspect of you I haven't seen yet." As we come closer to experiencing the essence of who we are, unmasked, we connect with our children.

Being honest about how we feel and expressing our heartfelt thoughts takes most of us out of our comfort zone. That's okay! When you feel the edge of your comfort zone, know you are headed for the connecting zone. *As you share your thoughts and feelings, your children will be better able to share theirs* and your connection will deepen.

Right in your own home, challenge yourself to follow your child's lead and learn to play again – their way. Just be present and allow them to take the lead. Since most parents have adopted the habit of organizing their child's play, this will probably take you out of your comfort zone. We're not used to *joining* their play. When we take the time to do so, however, the rewards are deep and rich, for both us and our child. Children marvel at the idea that they can teach us something, and we can learn so much from them. I love these words from George Benson's song, *The Greatest Love of All*: "Let the children's laughter remind us how we used to be."

I posted those words around my house as a reminder of what is truly important to me, when I found myself buried in diapers, or in my own sense of frustration at never being able to complete a chore without interruption! They helped to open my mind and heart, as my children reminded me how important it is to find joy in each and every moment.

§

"COME ON, MOM, run! It's fun!"

I looked at my three-year-old at the bottom of the hill smiling up at me, and thought, "There is no bloody way I am running down that hill! I'll break my neck." So instead, I carefully maneuvered my way down the embankment, lumbering slowly along until I caught up to where he was carefully examining his new-found caterpillar friend.

"Don't you like having fun?" asked Tyler as I knelt down beside him.

"Of course I like having fun," I replied, "I'm just not about to break my neck running down hills."

"I don't break my neck," Tyler replied simply. "It's fun."

Well, maybe breaking my neck *is* a slight exaggeration I thought to myself. And when is the last time I ran just for the fun of it anyway? It seemed like a very long time ago and I vowed that the very next hill Tyler ran down, I would follow him.

I didn't have to wait very long before my resolution was tested. Once again, Tyler ran laughing and giggling down to the bottom of the hill. "Come on, Mom! Run! It's fun!"

And so I did, and so it was! It was fast and effortless.

"When did I ever STOP running?" I asked myself.

And then I remembered. It was that Canada fitness program in grade 5. Somehow, try as I might, I could *not* pass the basic standard time for running around those barrels. I must have run that test ten times, but to no avail. Even though I had scored well in every other event, when it came time to determine the "medal" we would receive, I shall never forget my humiliation as the teacher called me up to receive the "red participation badge." My feet dragged as I hauled myself past my classmates down the long isle to receive my "reward." My face burned as I felt the snickers and silent jeering of my classmates as they dangled their gold, silver, and bronze medals in front of them, and I resolved quietly to myself that running was definitely not for me.

Ever since that day, I had gone out of my way to avoid running. Funny how I had become so wrapped up in past hurts, so busy in my serious adult life, and so worried about future scrapes and bruises, that I had denied myself the simple pleasures of life.

With the encouragement of my three-year-old son, I remembered the sheer joy and delight of effortless movement, and even today I rarely miss the opportunity to run – providing, of course, that it is indeed "downhill"!

§

Play is the foundation of bonding and connecting with your child. Dr. Fred Donaldson, in his book *Playing by Heart*, identifies play as the universal language. Play is the door to your child's heart and when you go through that door you *learn* how to be truly present with your child in the here and now.

Okay, so *when* are we going to connect?

Finding the time to talk with your children isn't always easy. When is *finding* time for anything easy? We have to *make* the time. Make it a habit. The half hour just before bedtime is a wonderful time to talk. Jack Canfield, co-author of *Chicken Soup for the Soul,* and renowned expert in building self-esteem says that the last half hour before sleep has 40 percent more impact on our day than any other period of time. Whatever happens then just keeps on working all night. Lying in bed beside your child before he or she goes to sleep is very non-threatening. Take turns talking about your favorite parts of the day and encourage kids to talk about anything that's bothering them. If they have something difficult to discuss, it is sometimes easier to discuss it in the dark.

Eye-to-eye communication is important in connecting with children. However, it is often misused. Before I knew better, I used to reprimand the kids I worked with. "Look at me when I'm talking to you," I'd say sternly when they'd done something "wrong." Somehow, I thought that boring the message of their wrongdoing into them would help them to understand how bad they had been, and then, of course, they'd act better. That turned out not to be the case, and I only needed to be reminded of how it felt to be on the receiving end to convince me to change my ways. I have come to understand that eye-to-eye communication is best reserved for those times when I am filling my children with love.

Driving in the car can be another ideal time to talk. You don't have to face each other and there is no escape. It gives you time and space to talk. Mealtimes are also important. Studies show a strong correlation between the family gathering and talking around the table, and children's success in life. Turn off the TV and the radio, light some candles, and make the dinner table an inviting place to be. You may find your family sitting and just talking long after the meal.

Your body speaks

Body language speaks louder than words. Sometimes, the best way to empathize with someone and to get him or her to open up is through body language. This can look like getting right down to the child's height when speaking with her, or slumping down beside her when she is slumped and miserable.

§

ONE MOTHER TOLD ME she was very concerned about her teenage son, who seemed depressed most of the time. It was hard for her to understand, as she was a bouncy, upbeat kind of person who always tried hard to focus on the positive. After our body language discussion, she decided to copy her son's body language and see what happened. The next day when her son came home from school and went into the kitchen, she gave him the milkshake she'd just made him. He collapsed in the chair, slumping over the kitchen table, one hand supporting his head, stirring the shake listlessly. She sat down next to him with her shake, mirroring his body language.

"The results were amazing," she reported excitedly to the class the next week. "It was like the floodgates opened and for the first time in our lives he shared what he was feeling. And I remembered just to listen." She was elated as the weeks went by and she saw her son gradually leave his depression behind, while their connection grew stronger and stronger.

§

Remember how we talked about feelings pointing to needs? Not long ago, a group of us were discussing what the need is when someone feels depressed. We agreed that the real need is for expression. The mom in the story above helped her son lift his depression by encouraging expression. The greatest encouragement of that expression was to mirror his body language, which allowed her to go to where he was at.

Sometimes, the fastest way to communicate to your child "I understand" is to show her through your body language that you know how she feels. By doing that, you probably *will* discover how she feels, because you'll *feel* it in your own body.

§

COLD AND MISERABLE after watching hockey game after hockey game, we jammed ourselves into a gray room – parents, kids, coaches, and all! The incessant whining of my three-year-old as she tugged at my pant legs was really getting on my nerves – almost as much as the commotion in the gray cement room. In exasperation, I squatted down to three-year-old height to see what her problem was. Instantly I understood my daughter's agitation. I had been feeling claustrophobic and penned in "up there." However, the confusion and stale air was doubly suffocating "down below" at three-year-old height. It had been frustrating enough "up above" simply trying to see over heads. "Down here" there was no hope of seeing over anyone and instead of one head; there were two legs to each body. No wonder my daughter felt miserable! Simply lifting her up helped, and I was reminded of the importance of seeing life through my daughter's eyes.

§

Pay attention to what your child is saying through his body language, as well as to what you are communicating through your body language. Albert Mehrabian's classic study breaks communication into three parts. *Communication*, he says, *is 55 percent body language; 38 percent tone of voice, and only 7 percent the actual words we speak.*

It is very confusing to a child if we send him mixed messages. Mixed messages occur when the three components above don't match.

Imagine you arrive home to find your partner viciously stirring "supper" on the stove. You don't even want to ask what "supper" is! Instead, you say, "Oh, honey, what's wrong?"

"Nothing!" she spats out vehemently.

Do you believe the words? Of course not! In fact, if your partner insists that nothing is wrong, you are likely to feel suspicious.

Meaningful communication happens when the words we speak are congruent with the message we send with our body and our tone of voice. Young children begin to distrust their own senses when we insist that nothing is wrong when something obviously is. We reduce stress and increase meaningful communication with others when we get in touch with how we really feel and learn to express it honestly.

Roadblocks to communication

Have you ever noticed that the biggest problems with communication often result from saying exactly the right thing to *shut down communication*? Sometimes saying nothing at all is better than the ways we've learned to help people – especially children – work through their problems.

The following story identifies some of the subconscious roles we assume when we try to help children with their problems. See if you recognize your own attempts to help others as you read the story. To understand why these approaches generally fail, put yourself into the shoes of the "lead character," Susan.

§

IT'S ALWAYS A STRUGGLE to get out the door on time on Monday mornings! "Why won't these kids help out?" Susan complained under her breath. "Cory, Kate! Let's go. Get your shoes, honey. Where are your shoes? Cory! What are you doing still in your pajamas?"

Five-year-old Cory just looked up at his mom defiantly. "Don't want to go to preschool!" he spat out.

"Well you're going," Susan shouted back at him. "Kate, oh good, you found your shoes. Okay, don't open the door yet! Don't open the door…"

Too late! Out scooted the new puppy, right between Kate's feet. "Snowball!" screamed Kate. "Oh no, Mommy, he'll get lost! We have to get him."

It seemed like it took forever to get out the door that morning. By the time they caught Snowball and Susan loaded them all into the car, she was already late for work – and she still had a 20-minute drive to get there! That is, 20 minutes if all went smoothly dropping the kids off, which, of course, it didn't. Cory wailed all the way to preschool, which Kate complained about non-stop, and Susan worried over the reaction of his teachers when they saw him in his pajamas. Then, Kate took forever getting out of the car, rifling through it in a last minute frenzy to find her spelling book.

"Oh great," thought Susan, "half an hour late and I'm exhausted – and I've just started the day!"

When Susan arrived at work, her boss was the first person to "greet" her. She took one look at her watch, cast an admonishing look Susan's way, and said simply, "Hope you've got that report finished for the meeting today."

"Report?" questioned Susan.

"Don't tell me you didn't get my message! I left it on your answering machine," came the brusque and rather cutting reply.

"Oh no," thought Susan, "now I remember! Oh well, I'll have to finish it at lunch."

But the rest of her day was just as hectic as the beginning and she didn't even have time to think about the report – until she was sitting in the 3 o'clock staff meeting. Now, of course, that was the only thing she *could* think about.

She spent an hour on pins and needles, waiting to be called. Just when she was beginning to think her boss might have forgotten, her boss turned to her and said firmly, "Susan, we'll have your report now."

Susan rose to her feet and started to apologize, "I'm sorry Ms. Murdock. I haven't quite fin…"

"It's not finished?!" interrupted her boss.

"Well, it's just that I've had quite a few emergencies lately…"

"You know, it seems to me," Ms. Murdock cut her off in mid sentence, "that you've had far too many emergencies lately young lady. Perhaps you'd better start thinking about your priorities! Your work doesn't seem to be one of them. Perhaps you can't really handle both your job and your family!"

"But," stammered Susan, "It's just that…"

"Save it," snapped Ms. Murdock. "Meeting adjourned!"

Susan stumbled back to her office, her stomach churning and her face stinging from the dozens of eyes she felt boring into her.

§

Now imagine that you are Susan as an entire parade of people comes by to "help" you. Go slowly through this section and give yourself time to really feel the impact of each "helper." How do you feel in each case?

The first to appear is PETUNIA PITIER herself: "Oh you poor thing! How are you *ever* going to handle this? To be spoken to like that, and in front of all your peers! I just don't know how I'd carry on if I were you!"

If you weren't feeling badly before, you probably are now! Never mind, because the next person to arrive has got some advice for you.

This is the ADVISOR: "Hey, if I were you, I wouldn't let her get away with that. I'd be in her office this minute giving her a piece of my mind. That's what you should do. You should march right in there and tell her exactly how you feel. You should be straight and you shouldn't hold back…"

Do you feel your anger rising with each additional "should"?

The next person has a friendlier voice, a softer voice to comfort you. It's the PHILOSOPHER: "Hey, it's not all that bad… Things will look better in the morning… Life can't always be a bed of roses you know!"

Are you ready to hear this now? Is it truly comforting? Let's hope so, because the next person isn't here to comfort you. He feels he has a personal stake in your career and your failure today has created a blemish on his career. After all, he is the person who recommended you to the company.

I'm talking about the GUILT-TRIPPER: "Now listen up, young lady," he begins, "just what do you think you're up to? You see these gray hairs? You put them there! I stuck my neck out for you and this is what I get in return? You'll be the death of me yet…"

On and on he goes until the clatter outside your door gives warning for everyone to clear out!

Enter the court: the JUDGE, the PROSECUTING ATTORNEY, and the DEFENSE. Oh! Not *your* defense, this guy has come to argue for the *boss!*

"It's not easy being a boss you know," begins the defense. "She has a lot of things to juggle. You've got to understand that if she's hard on you, it's because she has a lot of people to answer to…"

"Answer to," pipes up the prosecuting attorney. "That reminds me, young lady, just what *were* those emergencies that kept you from getting that report done? What could you possibly have to attend to that's more important than…"

"It's obvious," interrupts the judge, "that you really can't juggle both your job and your family. One of them will have to go."

You may be ready to throw the bench at all three of these guys, but the sound of the clickety-clack heels outside the door has got them on the run anyway.

Enter the COMMANDER-IN-CHIEF. She walks briskly over to you, looks down, and says, "Now don't you worry, honey. I'll take care of that old battle axe! Even if I have to take this to the media. She won't get away with this. I've been waiting for just the right opportunity to nail her! Let me handle this!"

Oh joy, now we'll really blow this scene up!

But wait! Enter Mr. ONE-UPMANSHIP, here to help you feel better by assuring you he has withstood far worse in his time: "Hey now, what's all the fuss about anyway? This isn't such a big deal! Why I remember one time when I was in my 20s. You wouldn't believe what my boss did to me…"

You may be feeling a little confused now. Here's the AMATEUR PSYCHOLOGIST to help you sort things through: "Hey, hey, hey," he says. "Now let's get to the heart of the matter here. This little episode isn't what's really troubling you. I think you're reflecting some deep-seated problems from your childhood. Perhaps it's the authority issue you have with your mother…"

"Step out of the way son," says a voice behind the amateur psychologist. "She couldn't have done anything else. Everybody has problems getting reports done. She shouldn't be blamed for this." This voice belongs to the RATIONALIZER. You may find the rationalizer comforting right now. However, if you are lured by this voice, you'll fall into a trap. The rationalizer excuses you from all responsibility. In the end, will that help? If you take no responsibility for your actions, you have no power in the situation.

In total confusion, you flop back into your chair, role your eyes, and spot a very welcome sight in your doorway.

Here is your VERY BEST FRIEND. Quietly, she walks over and sits down beside you. "Wow," she sighs deeply, "that was *some* meeting. I bet your feelings are churning right now. Kind of embarrassing, I bet, hey?" Then your friend does a most amazing thing. She closes her mouth and waits for you to talk!

Now, doesn't that one feel a lot different than all the rest? When we really put ourselves in the shoes of the person who needs help, it's so much easier to see what would be helpful. It's not that we don't ever want advice. Sometimes we need it and welcome it. Sometimes it helps to hear, "Things will look better in the morning." Sometimes it's great to have pull and help from the Commander-in-Chief types. But in the moment of emotional pain, what we really want and need is an understanding ear; someone *just to listen.* Someone with no other agenda except to be there for us, to help us clarify our feelings, and to validate them. We need someone who will get onside with us, believe in us, and support us in solving our own problems. That strengthens us.

In most of the scenarios above, the "helper" stepped between Susan and the problem, either condemning her or taking over for her. When will Susan learn to deal with her own problems? How will our *children* learn to problem-solve if we solve their problems for them, or if they have to spend their energy defending their right to be upset?

Do you see yourself taking any of those roles with your children? Here they are again:

- **THE PITIER:** "You poor thing! How are you *ever* going to handle this? I just don't know how I'd carry on if I were you!"

- **THE ADVISOR:** "If I were you… Here's what you should do… Make sure… Don't let him/her…"

- **THE PHILOSOPHER:** "Hey, it's not all that bad… Things will look better in the morning… Life can't always be a bed of roses you know!"

- **THE GUILT-TRIPPER:** "You're giving me gray hair… I'm going to have a heart attack if you don't stop…Don't you know how this hurts me…You kids will be the death of me yet!"

- **THE JUDGE:** "You will simply have to… It's obvious you can't handle this… That's it, you're just going to have to…"

- **THE PROSECUTING ATTORNEY:** "Well just what were you doing to make him/her so angry? Didn't you realize… You must have done something to deserve…"

- **THE DEFENSE:** (for the other side, of course) "Well, you just have to understand, it must have been difficult for him/her too… It can't be easy to be a teacher/boss/principal, etc."

- **THE COMMANDER-IN-CHIEF:** "Now don't you worry about one thing! I'll take care of this…"

- **ONE-UPMANSHIP:** "That's nothing! In my day… That reminds me of a time when I…"

- **THE RATIONALIZER:** "What else could you have done? It's not your fault."
- **AMATEUR PSYCHOLOGIST:** "Now let's get to the heart of the matter here. This little episode isn't what's really troubling you – I think you're reflecting some deep-seated problems from your childhood…"

If you discovered which roles you tend to play with your children, don't be dismayed. Rejoice! Awareness is a breakthrough in itself. You may even discover other roles you play that keep you from really connecting with and understanding your child.

Recently, I was listening to a speaker talk about showing compassion for ourselves. To illustrate her point she used two examples. In each case she asked what we would do or say to console the person with the problem. In the first example, a friend had the problem. People were quick to console the friend with words of understanding and empathy. In the second example, we were to imagine our child coming home with an "F" on a paper he'd worked hard to study for. Significantly, no one simply empathized with the child. The three people who responded all felt they needed to lecture the child, set up a new study schedule for him, or talk to the teacher and fix his problem for him. Everyone else seemed hard pressed to know what else to do. Why? It's because of conditioned parenting training. Even though we all knew that's not what our friend needed, somehow *we felt we had to step in and set the child straight*. This belief can destroy communication between parents and children.

These roles are like tapes that have been passed down from generation to generation and that play constantly inside our minds! Often, the words that roll out of our mouths are the very words we heard when we were a child. But we can catch them as that happens. *And* we can catch them inside our own minds!

Are you still carrying them with you and using them to beat yourself up? Maybe it's a subtle beating you give yourself. Many people suffer from self-criticism. (If we talked to our friends the way we talk to ourselves we wouldn't have any friends!) We're hard on ourselves, and then we pass those tapes on to our children, unless we make the conscious decision not to do so.

Sometimes it helps to share some of our own experiences and to talk person-to-person with our children. As long as we are not playing the one-upmanship game, children usually appreciate hearing about how we handled a bully, a cranky teacher, or a little sister.

Make a conscious decision now to show yourself and your children some compassion when encountering a difficult situation. Decide just to listen – to them, and to yourself. What is it they are really feeling? What is it *you* are feeling?

Remember that simply helping children to express uncomfortable emotions may be the only help they need in dealing with their problem. If more help is necessary, assume the support role in helping your child tackle the problem. Be onside with your child as you

- Listen soul-ly to understand. Set aside any urge to lecture.
- Acknowledge and identify feelings as you listen empathically.
- Demonstrate your belief in the child's ability to handle the issue, or teach her the skills needed to do so. Of course, you will have to step in if you believe her emotional or physical health and safety are threatened.

Teaching children to think

I had often heard the phrase, "Teach children how to think, not what to think," but I was not sure how to do that until I learned about Stephen Glenn's EIAG formula. (For a more detailed look at this method, see Chris Rush's program *Developing Capable People* or Stephen Glenn and Jane Nelson's book *Raising Self-Reliant Children in a Self-Indulgent World*. Simply put, when you talk with your child about an experience she's had, help her to

1. *Experience.* This is the event the child is reflecting on.
2. *Identify what happened.* Thinking back over an experience and relating the most important aspects of it can help her to put it into perspective. Be non-judgmental and ask open-ended questions to help her recall the event.

3. *Analyze what took place in terms of how this experience fits with other experiences in her life.* For example, if she is always rushing to get things done at the last minute, carefully and non-judgmentally help her to recognize developing patterns. You can ask her, "How do you think you ended up rushing like this? Help me understand how you plan your project." Explore how she feels about the situation. How does she get herself into these predicaments?
4. *Generalize about how she can learn from this experience to make future experiences more enjoyable.* Help her understand that it is for *her happiness and benefit* that she think about a better way to approach similar situations in the future. (Have you ever noticed that when we don't learn from one experience similar experiences keep repeating themselves over and over, often becoming more intensive?) Ask her what she can think of to do next time she has a project due. You can offer to help her in any way you can, but make it clear that she is ultimately responsible to make the changes she seeks.

You can help your child learn to think through issues using this formula, as well as develop the meaningful communication you'd like to have with her. *Every time children reflect on their own actions, organize and articulate what happened, and describe how it worked for them, they learn from their own experience and are truly learning how to think.*

Whose problem is it anyway?

Some of the confusion parents face around problem solving arises in the attempt to identify who owns the problem. The "simply listening" approach works beautifully when the child clearly owns the problem. Be aware, however, that if your child is accustomed to you solving her problems for her, there may be some initial discomfort as she insists that you continue to do so. Do not give in and solve her problem for her! Remain her sounding board as you maintain faith in her ability to create her own solution.

Sometimes it is not so obvious who owns the problem. Part of the challenge in parenting is to step back gradually and recognize when our child is ready to own the problem. For example, when children are babies and need to burp, parents need to take care of that. We get used to doing everything for them. As our children age, it takes keen observation and skill to step back and gradually let them take on more and more.

Generally, whoever is most upset owns the problem. But sometimes this is not clear, because when our child is upset it often triggers a strong response in us and we feel it is our responsibility to set matters straight. For example, if our child is upset because his sister doesn't want to play with him, it is not up to us to *make* her play with him. You can help him deal with his problem, but beware of taking on the responsibility of resolving it yourself. Empathize with him and help him move on to other alternatives. It is important that he learn to deal with his frustration. If you take the problem on as your own, you prevent him from learning what he needs to learn.

If a child comes home from school upset about the mark she received on an exam, she owns the problem. The parent's job is to listen to her and to help her resolve her own issue. It is not the parent's job to lecture or to run to the school and *make* the teacher change the grade. Punishing the child will only build resentment and prevents the child from taking responsibility for her own work.

If, on the other hand, you're upset because your 14-year-old comes home with an "unusual" haircut or hair color, you own the problem. It's his hair. It's not morally threatening and it's not unhealthy or life threatening. You can state how you feel about it, but any attempt to make him change his hair for you will meet with resistance, and he's likely to keep his hair like that for an extended period of time! Trying to make it his problem will only damage your relationship.

Sending whole messages
– when the parent owns the problem

Sometimes it's clear that the parent owns the problem. If we are upset because our child doesn't come to the table when called for lunch, *we* have the problem at that point. When we are upset, instead of getting angry and blaming the child for the situation, it's more effective and better-received if we send a whole "I message" to our child.

Instead of saying, "You always ruin supper hour by making us wait for you," try the following formula to express your concern:

When *(describe the behavior without judgment or blame)* _____

I feel *(name the emotion)* _____

Because *(be real and be honest)* _____

What I need is/what's important to me is _____

"When I call you to supper and you don't come right away, I feel frustrated because I want us all to eat together when the meal is hot. It's important to me that you let me know you've heard me and that you come right away."

Using such a formula can sound and feel awkward at first, but including these elements sends a whole message to your child and avoids a blame scenario that never resolves anything. Remember that sending or receiving a blaming statement evokes defensiveness and sets the power struggle in motion.

Sending whole messages helps us to clarify our own feelings and needs, and provides a healthy communication model for our children. The more real and honest we can be with our children, the better. For example, during a parenting class, one father expressed his frustration with his daughter, who was continually pinching her younger brother. His daughter could not be persuaded to stop, and threatening her had only made the situation worse. The whole message he put together in class was heartfelt and honest: "When you pinch your younger brother, I feel frustrated and helpless because it presses all of my buttons from when I was pinched and bullied as a child." The whole class felt the impact of that statement, and I bet his daughter did as well.

When parent & child both own the problem

Sometimes, simply stating our problem in the situation isn't enough. The problem may persist, or we may discover that our child has an issue with the situation at hand as well. For example, he may find it just too difficult to get up and leave his game the moment he's called to supper. Or it may be that he really *is* so engrossed in playing that he doesn't hear us call him. That's when *we need to put the problem on the table, consider it from both points of view, and work together to resolve it.*

Solution-finding technique

1. State the problem from your point of view using a whole "I message."
2. Listen to the child's point of view.
3. Once the problem has been clearly recognized, focus on finding a solution. Brainstorm possible solutions. It is important at this stage that all ideas be acknowledged and accepted. Children must have input and an investment in the solution if problem solving is to work.
4. Together, select a course of action from the alternatives generated.
5. Commit to trying a selected alternative for a defined time period. (The younger the child, the shorter the time period selected.)
6. Evaluate effectiveness after the agreed upon time period.

With persistent and ongoing problems, letting your child know in advance what you'd like to discuss, then sitting down with a pen and paper sometime later, can be especially effective. Even young children – *especially* young children who can't yet read and write – are impressed that Mom or Dad would take the time to write down their ideas. Posting a record of the agreed-upon solution where children can see it helps everyone to focus on the solution.

৯

TEMPER TANTRUMS were a major issue in Karen's family. After hearing about the problem-solving technique, she chose a good time to talk with her daughter and they sat down to discuss the problem together. Karen told her daughter, "When you scream and yell and get so upset, I feel frustrated and miserable because it's hard on my ears and bothers my nerves. You don't look very happy either. What happens when you get so upset?"

"Don't know," replied three-year-old Kaley. "Can't help it."

"Well, maybe we can think of some ways that we can make things better for both of us," suggested Karen, "because you're not happy, and it's hard on everyone when you start screaming. I've got some paper here, and as we think of things you can do to keep from screaming all the time, we can write them down, okay?"

Kaley was wide-eyed and impressed that her mother was going to write down what she said. "Okay," she said.

"So I'm going to write down every idea you and I can think of that will help us deal with your temper tantrums," said Karen. "Can you think of something that can help?"

"Don't like the boys," said Kaley. "Tell them to go away." Karen wrote it down: "Tell boys to go away."

"Maybe I could leave the house when you start to scream," suggested Karen and started to write it down.

"No," protested Kaley, "don't want you to leave." Karen reminded her she was just writing down every idea that came to mind and then they would choose together which one to try.

"I could leave," suggested Kaley.

"Maybe we could do an 'angry dance' to shake the anger out before you get so mad you can't stop screaming," Karen suggested.

They continued to brainstorm ideas like screaming into a pillow, throwing her stuffed toys, and using her brother as a punching bag. (Yes, they wrote that down, too, and it added a bit of humor to their brainstorming session!) When they couldn't think of any more ideas, they looked back on the ones they had. *That* was when Karen said she couldn't agree with Kaley using her brothers as a punching bag. Kaley told her the ones that wouldn't work for her and stroked them off the list.

They finally decided that since Kaley liked to scream and stomp when she was upset, as soon as she felt herself getting mad, she could go onto the deck and do an "anger dance." (Sometimes you just can't worry about how thrilled the neighbors will be with you!) They posted their agreement at Kaley's eye level on the sliding glass door that led to the deck. Before each mealtime, they'd check in together to see how she was doing with managing her temper tantrums.

Karen was amazed at how deciding on a method of dealing with Kaley's anger, and the attention given to her success in managing her temper tantrums, seemed to give Kaley more control over them. When she *did* have a tantrum after that, Kaley was happy that her mom could still witness it, and the whole family was relieved to have a sound barrier.

§

Einstein said, "*No problem can be solved at the level at which it was created.*" Lift yourself above the problem and *once the problem is defined, remain focused on solutions!* Do not go over and over different aspects of the problem. Doing so will only turn your conversation into a "blame session" and nothing will be resolved. The brainstorming session is all about solutions. Selecting and implementing a course of action focuses on the solution. Evaluating its effectiveness is done with the intent of finding another solution if the current one isn't working.

Some problems are long-standing and reoccurring. It can take time, patience, and maturity to work through them. There are no "quick fixes," but it can sure help to bring problems out into the open and work at finding the solutions together. Sometimes we expect our children to be able to resolve problems beyond their maturity level. In the next chapter, we'll look at the impact our expectations have on our children.

Involving our children in the problem-solving process is the most likely way to ensure that they will buy into the solution. This process sets the stage for increased cooperation in our home, and can create an environment where even family chores are more palatable.

Household chores:
why won't these kids cooperate & help me?

Sometimes, even when we take time to work through problems together, it's still difficult to get kids to help around the house. All the skills in the world won't help you to motivate your child to cooperate with you unless you are truly present with him. Get into his space in a friendly way, capture his attention with your loving eye contact, and entice him to connect with you. Dr. Gordon Neufeld talks about the importance of "wooing" your child and thereby strengthening the attachment bond between you. In essence, it is the strength of this attachment that gives your child the greatest encouragement and that motivates him to cooperate and to invite your influence into his life.

"Collect before you direct," Neufeld would say. So often, we are simply directing orders at our child. Before simply issuing an order, however, it is important to connect with your child. Some families live together for years with out really connecting. They brush by one another in the hallway and hardly acknowledge the other's presence. You'll notice a big difference in the level of cooperation in your home when you take time to truly connect.

You can gain children's cooperation around household chores by inviting them to work with you. Now, if you are miserable and out of sorts doing the chores, it will not be a very exciting invitation. Take stock of your own attitude.

I recall one evening when I was especially "into" cleaning up the kitchen. I was puttering about happily, when my 9-year-old daughter asked if she could join in. We had a great time laughing and talking, and yes, cleaning! She said, "You know, Mom, I didn't know this could be fun."

That started me thinking about how often I had sent the message that chores were unpleasant, but had to be done. From that day, I became more conscious about my own attitude and have since tried hard to make it more of an invitation to the kids to help. Now we often clean up together, talking and joking and enjoying the time, rather than arguing over whose turn it is to do the dishes.

Children may be more likely to pitch in and help when everyone's working together. Sometimes working in the same room helps. The most productive cleaning times around our house are when we've got a common goal, such as leaving for downtown in an hour. We divide the tasks up together and everyone works at the same time. When everyone is finished, we all get to leave.

Make sure children understand how to do a task assigned to them and are not overwhelmed by it. Adults often forget that simple things take training, and assume their child knows what to do. The next chapter gives you a method of encouraging children to learn new tasks.

Summary

Kids are people first – and parents are people first, too! Talking with your child, person to person, is essential to developing meaningful communication and cooperation in your home. Maintain a non-judgmental, open, and curious attitude about your child.

Stop using the "roadblocks" to communication and appreciate each stage of growth your child passes through. Help him learn *how to think*, not *what to think*.

Become aware of body language, for it can help you to understand your child and to communicate your messages without generating defensiveness. Mixed messages are confusing. The content of what you say must match your tone of voice and body language.

Send whole, complete messages to your child, when you are

expressing a problem you have. Learn to identify who owns the problem. Work together on problems you both own together. As soon as you have identified the problem from all perspectives, focus on the solution.

Maintain an attitude of working together to solve problems and to take care of family chores. It is our own attitude that sets the example. Invite children to cooperate and to resolve issues peacefully.

The Way of Encouragement

Raising Resilient, Self-Motivated, & Responsible Individuals

Model the courage to be imperfect.

A bruised knee will heal; bruised courage may last a lifetime.
— RUDOLF DREIKURS

Never do for the child what he can do for himself.
— RUDOLF DREIKURS

A BOY FROM INDIA was studying under a Master to learn life's secrets. One day, this boy found a cocoon and ran excitedly to his Master to tell him about it. "How can I learn from this, Master? What should I do?"

The Master said to the boy, "Simply observe. Watch carefully as the butterfly emerges. Do nothing else; simply watch."

The boy ran back to the cocoon and watched and watched. Eventually, he noticed a long thin crack developing throughout the length of the cocoon. He waited excitedly as he saw one hairy leg push its way through the crack, then another, and another. Slowly, one wing broke away from the cocoon, and then another leg. But now the butterfly appeared to be stuck. Struggle as it may, the second wing clung stubbornly to the inside of the cocoon. The boy, unable to endure the anxiety of watching the butterfly's struggle, reached into the cocoon, freed the wing, and pulled the butterfly out.

The butterfly fluttered into the air for a brief moment, then spiraled down to the earth. It was unable to fly.

The boy was heartbroken. He ran to his Master, saying, "Master, Master, something is terribly wrong! I did just as you said and it was exciting to watch the butterfly come out of the cocoon, but now it can't fly. What happened?"

"Are you sure you *only* watched?" queried the Master.

"Well, I *did* help it a little," explained the boy. "It was having so much trouble freeing its last wing, I reached in to pull it out."

"It is difficult to watch the struggle," explained the Master, "but when you reached in to pull the butterfly out, you denied it the opportunity to strengthen its own wings. That is why it can't fly."

§

After hearing that story, I certainly did some thinking and re-evaluating around how much I did for my kids. Author Rudolf Dreikurs says, "Never do for a child what he can do for himself." But, gee whiz, who has the patience to wait for their child to tie his shoes every time they go out? Most the time it's easier to do it yourself! And what about getting it *right* – I mean, sure my daughter can fix her own hair, but look how she fixes it! What will people say? What will people think? Will they think I don't care – or, horror of horrors, will they think I fixed her hair like that?

Helping children develop courage

There are many reasons why we do things for our children, even if they can do them for themselves. Sometimes it's just too difficult to watch our children struggle with life's challenges. We love them so much and we want their lives to be trouble free. When we "fix" their problems for them, we believe we are doing what is best for them. But while children do need help with some of the very difficult issues that they face, too often we deny them the opportunity to "strengthen their own wings."

Encouragement is one of the most precious gifts we can give our children because it is about helping our children develop the courage, spirit, and ability to meet life's challenges. To develop these qualities, however, children must have the need to find them and use them.

The instinct to protect children from all harm is so strong that sometimes we end up preventing them from developing the courage and tools they need to live their lives. Author Stephen Glenn says that we are the only species that actually puts our young at risk by keeping them from all danger, and from developing the skills to deal with danger. Just watch a mother lion – she'll take her cubs out and watch from nearby as they tackle the challenges of survival.

Being a parent is a tough job. We do need to watch for the safety of the children in our care. Equally important, however, is encouraging them to take risks. One of my favorite quotes comes from Rudolf Dreikurs: *"A bruised knee will heal; bruised courage may last a lifetime."*

We all need to take calculated risks in this lifetime. Without taking these risks, we rob ourselves of the opportunity to develop a sense of trust in ourselves and in the universe.

It may be that, as a child, you were not allowed to take such risks. If this is true, then you likely know the pain that comes from living in the fear of being hurt, or of making a mistake. It will take courage for you to allow yourself and your children to make mistakes. Start small. Little by little, step back and gradually take on more and more challenges. When children are small, the playground is a good place to start. Let them take the lead. Follow them to see what they want to try. *Be their safety net, but let them go!* Gradually, you can back off.

If a child is especially timid or fearful about trying new things, the most precious gift you can give her is the courage to try or the courage to keep going, even in the face of past failures.

I once listened to a psychologist talk about the importance of taking risks. She said that, essentially, there are two attitudes we choose between in this life: One is, "Nothing ventured, nothing gained." The other is "Nothing ventured, nothing lost." The first is an attitude of encouragement, the second an attitude of discouragement.

The attitude your child will carry in life has a great deal to do with the attitude you yourself adopt. Do you give yourself permission to make mistakes? Do you have the courage to try something new, even when there is no guarantee of "success"? Thomas Edison reportedly tried 2000 different materials before he discovered the filament for the light bulb. A reporter interviewing him asked, "How could you keep going in spite of so many failures?" He replied, "There were no failures! I learned from every single experiment. I needed every single one of those 'failures,' as you call them, to discover the right one."

Perhaps our biggest problem with problems is the way we look at them – as something we need to rid our lives of. When I was growing up, I didn't really see adults having problems, and so I believed that one day I would magically grow out of mine. Later, when I was 22 years old, I was cleaning rooms at the university for a summer job. My cleaning partner was a woman in her early 60s. One day she came to work very upset and started to share all of the problems she was having in her relationship. I ended up crying with her, but to be honest, it wasn't all empathy. I cried because I realized that I would probably never grow out of my problems. Today, I know that the objective of life is not to grow out of problems, or to have someone move in and sweep them all away. Instead, it is most helpful to view problems as "opportunities in work clothes."

Problems are opportunities in work clothes!

Creative problem solving is a skill we learn and develop through practice, and it is perhaps the most important tool that we can give our children. It requires that our children *learn to face life's troubles with courage and confidence in their own abilities.* So how can we teach courage and confidence?

It is our job as parents to deepen our own strength and belief in the value of learning through life's experiences, so that we will know how and when to step aside and allow our children to develop their own strength and ability to solve the problems that come their way. *Before we leap to fix their problems, we need to ask ourselves, "Does my child need support with this issue, and if so, how can I support her without taking over?"*

If we look before we leap, we may see strengths in our children that surprise us. Identifying those strengths and relating them specifically and accurately to our children can give them great encouragement. It may be something as simple as watching our toddler search for a way out from underneath the table. Instead of clearing a pathway for him, we can watch, coaching him if necessary: "Oh, it is so frustrating when that big doll is right in your pathway! How else can you get out from under there? Can you figure out how to back up?" You many need to get down with him and coach him to back up. Show him you believe in his ability to develop the strength and ability to deal with whatever issues come his way. Start with the "small stuff" and help him to develop awareness and belief in himself and his abilities.

Helping children develop inner qualities

Dr. William Glasser once said, "Children will find in the eyes of the parents and teachers who raise them, mirrors in which they discover themselves." If we look for our children's specific strengths and abilities, we can give them powerful feedback on the abilities they already possess to meet life's challenges.

> "Children will find in the eyes of the parents and teachers who raise them, mirrors in which they discover themselves."
>
> – William Glasser

Greatest strength, greatest weakness

Sometimes we have to search beneath the surface to recognize our child's strengths, because *strengths often come disguised as weaknesses.* Have you ever heard the saying, *"Greatest strength, greatest weakness"*? Frequently, what bothers us most about someone in a certain situation is also what we like at a different time, in a different situation. A famous psychologist once said, "Tell me why you married him and I'll tell you why you're divorcing him. You married him because he was the life of the party and now you're divorcing him because he won't leave a party! Or maybe you married him because he was solid, upright and stable and you're divorcing him because he's boring, uptight and stale!"

Think about the many traits that can be perceived as positive or negative, depending upon the circumstances.

Troublesome Trait	Viewed as a Strength
stubborn	persistent, determined
overly talkative	friendly, informative
bossy	responsible, in control
nosy	inquisitive
wishy-washy	flexible
socially aggressive	exciting, fun
lazy	easygoing, relaxed
outspoken	not afraid to speak up

Notice that many of the same actions are viewed as an asset when demonstrated by an adult, but when a child does the same thing, they are often perceived negatively. For example, if an adult asks someone to blow her cigarette smoke in another direction, he is seen as assertive. If a child does the same thing, he is often seen as insolent. If an adult knocks something over, she had an "accident"; too often, if a child knocks something over, she is "clumsy." An adult is "selective" about what she eats; a child is "picky."

If we can remember that the characteristics that drive us crazy in our children are traits and abilities we come to admire in adult life, it helps us to teach our children how to use such traits as strengths.

§

CAMPING WITH THE KIDS can be a challenge at any age. It was very close to suppertime when Elaine and David and their three children – aged six, four, and two – pulled into the most amazing campground. There was a wide variety of campsites to choose from. Everyone was hungry and excited, although a bit cranky from the hot drive. As they searched about for just the right spot, they became more and more confused. No one knew which one to choose – except for the oldest, the six-year-old. He knew *exactly* which one he wanted. Trouble was, the one he wanted was the only one his younger brother really *didn't* want to stay in, because it was dark and scary. The struggle was on. The more the youngest didn't want to stay there, the more the oldest insisted that they must. Elaine heard herself muttering inside her head about how stubborn their eldest was, and then reminded herself to see the positive side of "stubborn."

Sitting down next to Devon in the van, she began, "You know what, Devon? Out of the whole family, you're the only one who really knows which camping spot you want. That's a real strength." Devon looked at her a little suspiciously, she thought, but she kept going. "And not only that, but once you decide on what you want, you really stick with it. You have a lot of determination and persistence." Devon was really interested in the conversation now. "And that persistence and determination and ability to make decisions about what you want will really help you all your life, *if…*" (and here Elaine paused)…

"If what, Mommy?" Devon asked, right on cue.

"*If* you know when it's important to persist and hang

on to what you want, and when to let go and choose something else. And right now, Devon, your brother doesn't want to stay in that camping spot, and there are lots of other beautiful ones. So this is a time to let go and choose another!"

Elaine wasn't sure if Devon really understood all of that, but he certainly seemed to, because he said, "Oh, okay, how about that one over there?"

Elaine recalls thinking what a different conversation it would have been if she had taken the usual "Devon-don't-be-so-stubborn" route.

§

Letting our children know we appreciate the positive side of their characteristics and helping them to learn when to use their strengths and when these strengths create problems for them *and* for us, gives them essential interpersonal life skills, builds their esteem, and opens our relationship with them.

The Great Expedition...

Begin today to look for and reflect back to your child, her qualities, strengths and abilities.

A life-changing exercise for a number of parents I've worked with has been to go home and search for 50 qualities in each of their children. When they've discovered those, their next task is to find 50 qualities within themselves.

Here are some qualities to search for. Feel free to add your own!

Qualities and Abilities

conscientious	gentle	communicative
enterprising	self-disciplined	effective negotiator
ingenious	self-motivated	sincere
intelligent	thoughtful	honest
strong	crafty	expressive
resourceful	resilient	organized
dependable	encouraging	decisive
thorough	articulate	fair
optimistic	sense of humor	understanding
focused	investigative	trustworthy
caring	inspirational	competent
empathetic	logical	thrifty
loving	reliable	generous
intuitive	efficient	loyal
hard working	interesting	patient
persistent	clever	insightful
tenacious	dramatic	meticulous
agile	careful	diligent
flexible	precise	listener
adaptable	imaginative	punctual
musical	respectful	original
easygoing	observant	open-minded
artistic	cooperative	analytical

Notice that these are qualities and abilities we can all develop as human beings. None of these words are judgmental. Each of them gives specific information rather than reflecting a qualitative judgment (such as good, wonderful, fantastic, etc.).

Praising isn't necessarily encouraging

Most parents believe that they are encouraging their children when they lavish praise on them. "What a good girl!" "Aren't you wonderful!" "That's a magnificent picture."

Unfortunately, such judgmental praising can have a rebound effect. "Now hold on here," many parents protest when this subject comes up. "Are you telling me that when I praise my kid for being good, I'm not encouraging him?"

It's possible – in fact, *praise can often keep children from developing the courage and tools they need to meet life's challenges. Praise can hook kids on needing outside approval in order to feel good about themselves.* Telling children how pleased and proud we are of them, and how good they are, without giving them information about their specific strengths can turn them into people-pleasing, approval-seeking junkies. We are inadvertently sending a message to them that "other people's opinions of me are more important than my own."

Just think about the impact of that belief on one's life! Imagine dealing with peer pressure, important decision-making situations, and intimate relationships if that belief runs your life. Many people understand this all too well, for many of us were raised with that belief and have experienced the turmoil it has created in our own lives. Roger Mellot, a stress specialist, identifies the need for the approval from others as one of the two underlying causes of stress. The other is the need for control. Parents get a double whammy here, because they often feel a need to control their child and the need for their child's approval all at the same time. Essentially, this boils down to, "Look kid, I need to control you, but I want you to approve of me controlling you, all right?" Controlling children through praise and reward is a method of "child rearing" and "classroom management" that teachers and parents have been using for generations.

Years ago, as a teacher, I went to professional development day workshops and came away with stickers and books with a thousand and one ways to say "fantastic, wonderful, terrific, you're the best," and other loaded, judgmental statements. We were taught that this would motivate kids – and it can, *as long as the child still wants* your *approval, and the reward is enticing enough.* But a strange thing happens as children approach their teen years. Suddenly they're more interested in their peer's approval than in yours. Peer pressure becomes a major stress in their lives. Is that what you as a parent want?

Not only that, but if parents have been rewarding children with candy every time they use the potty, chances are good that as the children get older they'll demand bigger rewards than that.

So now we have people-pleasing junkies who seem ungrateful and demanding! Isn't that the flip side of parents who need control and want approval all at the same time?

"But rewards work!" some parents exclaim in exasperation. "Rewards get my child to do what I want him to do."

Before insisting that rewards "work," please reread those last few paragraphs and consider, "Does this 'work' in light of my Vision Statement for my family?"

Consider this: How often do you feel uncomfortable with praise in your own life? What if you believe the praise is insincere? Imagine you've hauled yourself out of bed in a hurry, rushed down to the store in an emergency (You're out of coffee creamer!) and run into your son's teacher. She looks at you and says, "You always look so fantastic! How do you do it?" What are you thinking?

Or suppose you're golfing for the first time with your boss and his friends. Normally, you're not a great golfer, but on the first drive you send the ball down the fairway and onto the green. "Wow, what a pro! That was a perfect shot!" The others look at you in amazement. Do you feel pressured to keep it up? How do you feel if it's all downhill from there?

Or how do you feel when you've spent hours rearranging furniture, cleaning and decorating, and your partner hardly glances at the room upon entering. You ask, "What do you think?" The answer is short, hurried, and sweet: "Oh, it's great, honey! Terrific!" Do you feel like he has really noticed and appreciated your work?

How do you feel when you're attending a class and the instructor has lavished praise on several students, but not on you? I know I grew up believing I had absolutely no artistic talent, because my cousin was the "artist" in the group. I remember clearly my aunt lavishing praise on her as I sat close by. On and on she went, at least that's how it seemed to me, about my cousin's beautiful pictures and her amazing artistic talent. Then, she'd notice me sitting there and assure me, "Of course, that's nice, too, dear!" My aunt wasn't trying to make me feel bad. In fact, I'm sure it never entered her mind that she'd had any impact on me at all. And I said nothing. I simply went inside and sadly affirmed to myself that I could not color, or draw. It wasn't until I was 32 and *had* to take an art class to complete my degree that I was able to revisit that belief and shift it. Today, art fills my life with joy.

As other children watch you lavish praise on one child, the onlookers often receive the message that their work is inferior. Praise can affect children in different ways. Children might feel they have to excel every time, or not try at all; or they may feel that the praise is insincere and be suspicious about our motivation for giving it to them. The saddest consequence of using praise alone is that it can keep our kids hooked on a need for approval, and it can keep us from truly coming to know our children and what their strengths are.

Letting go of reward & praise, & entering your child's heart

Praising and rewarding were tough parental "tools" to let go of – until I learned how to truly encourage my children. Then, I learned how to be a mirror to them, searching for their strengths and reflecting those strengths back to them so that they could see them too. In my efforts to be specific about their strengths, I had to get truly involved with my children, and that opened the door to being present with them. As Roger Mellot, in his audiobook *Stress Solutions for Professionals*, says, *"Being present is the entrance exam to getting into a child's heart. Sadly, that's why many parents never ever get to know their children, even though they live with them for years."*

Here are some tools to help you enter your child's heart, to help you stay present with your child and to help her to understand her strengths and abilities. These tools will help her develop persistence and the determination to move toward her own goals, to trust her intuition and to know her own heart. They will help your child have the necessary strength and belief in herself to withstand peer pressure and to act from her deepest sense of what's right.

1. Be present and become involved in your child's process (whatever she is doing). Actively search out what *is* working.
2. Describe what you see. Be specific and avoid judgment.
3. Express your feelings and/or appreciation.
4. Point out specific strengths, characteristics, and inner qualities your child is demonstrating.
5. Let your child praise herself!

> The saddest consequence of using praise alone is that it can keep our kids hooked on a need for approval, and it can keep us from truly coming to know our children and what their strengths are.

You can use this process anytime you notice your child doing something that reflects an inner strength. You can also use it when you want to encourage your child in an activity, but are unsure of how to proceed: for example, when your child brings you her latest artwork to admire and you are unsure of which way to hold the page! It may look like a lot of scribble and you may be tempted to simply say, "Oh how beautiful," and to think that she will find that encouraging. After all, you want to avoid hurting her feelings. Unfortunately, you will also avoid taking the time to become involved and to really *look* at her work. How often have we been too busy with our own "stuff" to shift our attention and really look? When that happens too often, we miss out on being truly present with our children, and so we fail the entrance exam into their hearts.

If you want to pass that entrance exam and let your child know you are truly with her, apply the encouragement tools I've just described. Using the example of the child's artwork, above, you can

1. *Take the attitude of wanting to get involved* and get ready to point out what works. Adopt a non-judgmental, curious attitude, and determine to search for strengths.
2. *Describe what you see.* "Oh, look at this. I see you went dot, dot, dot here, and around and around in a circle there. Then zig, zig, zig over here. You've used blue on top and green below." (Avoid labeling and naming things trees, grass, etc. Young children often draw simply for the pleasure of putting marks on the paper and it doesn't need to represent anything in particular.)
3. *Tell her how you feel.* "It makes me feel happy just to look at this picture."
4. *Name her inner qualities.* "You're really getting very adventurous with the colors and different lines."
5. *Let your child praise herself.* Chances are good your child will nod happily, add a few words of her own, and run off to do some more.

I offer these tools only to help you understand *how* you can fully appreciate and acknowledge your child's abilities and strengths. You don't have to include each of these steps every time. Simply describing is often enough to get *you* involved and to encourage your child to do more. It also helps to build vocabulary. I remember listening to my boys one day describing their latest Lego project to a friend of mine. I was astounded at their vocabulary, which I knew had developed so extensively because they had listened to me "describe what I'd seen" so many times.

Eventually, you will want your child to be able to identify her own strengths. Often, the highest form of encouragement is to ask your child to tell you about her picture and what she likes about it. Or ask your child to tell you about how he finally managed to solve the problem he'd been working on. Or get her to share with you how she managed to tell her best friend the truth, and still show her she cared. There are a thousand and one scenarios that happen in our child's life, and every time they get something to work for them, we can help them strengthen their understanding of the process and the strengths they used, so that they are more prepared to meet other challenges.

The language of encouragement

Your sincerity and desire to connect with your child is crucial. Without your desire to connect, no tools or phrases can help you. Your presence, coupled with your desire to reflect your child's specific strengths and abilities, is far more important than memorizing "steps" or specific phrases. However, many people find examples helpful when trying to grasp new concepts. Therefore, here are some phrases that may help you to show confidence in your child, focus on his contributions, and recognize effort and improvement.

Showing confidence in your child

- "Knowing you, I'm sure you'll figure this out. Look what you've already done…"
- "I have confidence in your judgment."
- "I'm sure that you'll make the decision that is right for you."
- "Boy that's a tough one, but I'm sure you'll work it out."
- "You'd like me to think you can't do it, but I have faith in you; you'll get it!"
- "You did that all by yourself? Wow! You really are getting independent. You're growing up fast!"
- "How do you think we should tackle this problem?"

Focusing on contribution, assets, and appreciation

- "Thanks, that was a big help when you…"
- "It was so thoughtful of you to…"
- "You sure made my job easier. Thanks for your help with…"
- "I couldn't have done it without you."
- "I really enjoyed today because… Thanks!"
- "You have a lot of skill in… Would you do that for the family?"
- "I really enjoy your laughter/ singing/ helpfulness, etc."
- "I really appreciate it when you take the initiative, see what needs to be done, and do it! You've made my day so much easier – thanks!"
- "I love you, and nothing can ever change that!"

- "You're a really amazing person. I'm sure glad you're my son/daughter."
- "Remember, it's you I love, not your grades."

Recognizing effort and improvement

- "Wow! That's really coming along. Last time I saw your project…"
- "I know it seems like you're moving slowly, but just think back to when you started. See how far you've come. Remember when…?"
- "I can see you're improving in… (Be specific)."
- "You really gave it a good try! Tell me what you've learned through all this."
- "It looks as if you spent a lot of time thinking that through."
- "You're almost there. I know you're tired, but hang in there."
- "You're getting better at…"

Parents sometimes say they feel uncomfortable repeating these phrases to their children. Their words don't sound and feel natural. I can relate. And if you can simply remember to be present and to express your appreciation of your child's specific qualities, that may be all the guidance you want or need. If, however, you've grown accustomed to praising your child without truly acknowledging him, these phrases provide concrete examples of how and where you can begin to make changes. Be gentle with yourself. It takes time and practice. What doesn't? Think of any new skill you've learned. The first time you held a golf club and learned the "proper" golf swing it probably didn't feel natural either, especially if you had fallen into the habit of swinging it your own way. If you want to be a really good golfer, however, you will take the time to deal with the initial discomfort and practice until it becomes comfortable. The same holds true for using this new skill of encouragement.

So what do you do if one of those judgmental "praise" words slips out? Don't panic! There is no need to correct yourself. When you *do* praise your child, simply add the details explaining why you thought she was "good."

Some children need to be "weaned" off praise. Praise can become very addictive. Some children may protest when you first stop using it, and actively seek out your approval more and more. "Mommy, aren't I a good girl anymore?" "Daddy, aren't you proud of me? Are you, Daddy, are you?"

Let your child know that, of course, you are proud of him. But it's more important that he be proud of himself. Ask him to tell you about his project or activity and what he thinks worked for him. Give him the reasons you are proud of him. Gradually, as you focus on specific strengths and abilities, he won't need you to speak the praise; he'll praise himself as he discovers his own talents and abilities.

Praise & encouragement – what's the difference?

Praise	Encouragement
Focuses on the end result. Effect: Child learns to focus on the end result. Winning is everything!	Focuses on step-by-step improvement. Effect: Child learns persistence, to enjoy the process, and to stay in the moment.
Compares child with others. Child learns he is only good if he is better than someone else. Often results in rivalry and competition.	Gives full attention to child without comparison to others. Child learns to appreciate and know herself. There is no competition because there is no judgment. Creates an atmosphere of cooperation.
"Good girl" can be wiped out with "Bad girl" only moments later.	Child knows specifically what she has done well. Nothing can take that away.

Keeps child hooked on other people's opinions.	Teaches child to value her own opinions and judgments.
Child becomes extrinsically motivated. They will only do something in exchange for a reward.	Child becomes intrinsically motivated to develop strengths and talents, and to use them.
Is easy to dish out without thinking. Sometimes received as phony or insincere.	Takes time and thought to be encouraging. To encourage another, one must become involved.
It's like fast food. It provides a quick fix but it doesn't nourish the development of the child.	Like a fine, nurturing meal, it can take time to prepare but it provides lasting nourishment to the child and stimulates healthy growth.

Take time for training

My daughter recently made a very astute observation. She said, "You know, Mom, some teachers only tell you what you did wrong. But they don't tell you how to do it right. What good is that?"

Most people think we teach best by pointing out what's not working. The truth is we teach best by pointing out specifically what *is* working. Pointing out what's working requires a huge shift in perception for most of us, who've been trained to look for what's wrong and ignore what's right. Think of how discouraging this is in your own world.

Imagine having worked hard to make a special dinner for your partner. Everything is perfect – or almost, except for the carrots which have a distinctly burnt flavor. Oh, and you didn't exactly clean up the kitchen according to your partner's standards. Now imagine your partner sits down to dinner and the only comments are, "What'd you do to the carrots?" and "Couldn't you at least have wiped the counters?"

How would you feel about surprising your partner with another dinner? Would you feel encouraged to "clean up your act and get it right next time"? I doubt it.

Some of you don't have to imagine this – you've lived it! Perhaps you're living it now. If so, how do you feel about it? Does that kind of behavior help your relationship? What does it do for your self-esteem?

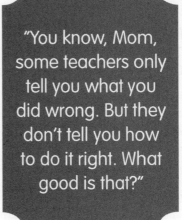

"You know, Mom, some teachers only tell you what you did wrong. But they don't tell you how to do it right. What good is that?"

But let's say your partner comes in the door, sits down and starts to describe everything he or she appreciates about the dinner you've prepared. What if they even tell you how they appreciate your thoughtfulness and creativity? Is it possible that you'd be encouraged to continue to surprise your partner?

We gain cooperation by focusing on what's working. We can also teach what's right by describing what's working.

Imagine your six-year-old comes home from school with a page of "a's" that looks like this. How encouraged and motivated will he be to try harder and practice more if you simply X out each "a" that's not right? However, what if you zero in on the "a" that "works"? See how round the circle is? The stick is straight up and down and is nicely attached. The whole "a" sits between the lines.

&

WHEN KATE was first learning this skill, she walked into the disaster area her son called his bedroom and clamped her mouth shut before the usual tirade of words passed through it. (You know: "Look at this mess! Just look at this mess! I can't even see the bed. Jared, get in here and pick these clothes up, make your bed, put your toys away, clean off your dresser…) Instead, Kate searched for *something* that was in order. It took some time before her eye spotted Jared's rock collection, arranged carefully and neatly on one corner of his dresser.

Kate stepped gingerly through the toys and clothing and as she approached the dresser, she said, "Oh, Jared, look at this! These rocks are a pleasure to look at. You've arranged them in a very neat and interesting way. You really know how to organize the things you care about, don't you?"

Jared beamed and said, "Yeah, I guess I do – and I can make the rest of the dresser look good too!" (Now Kate was beaming as well!)

As Jared learned to see himself as organized, and learned some of the tools to keep himself organized (like grouping and arranging similar items together), he became more organized. There was a time in his life when Kate was quite concerned about his lack of organizational ability. Today, however, his room is possibly the most organized of the household, and he keeps himself on task and schedules his time wisely.

§

Next time your child cleans up his room, go on a "what's working" mission. Determine before you open the door that you will look for and point out (describing non-judgmentally) what's in order. Then ask yourself if your child needs some training, in order to keep his room clean and neat.

Keep a sharp eye out at all times for the behavior you want to see in your child. Zoom in on that and give it your *attention*. Remember: children will get their parents' attention one way or the other. Proactively searching for the positive and giving attention to that not only encourages more of that kind of behavior, it reduces the need for children to "act out" to get parental attention.

Break tasks into manageable steps

Are you assuming your child knows how to do things simply from watching you? Does she really know how to make her bed, put away her toys, or wash the dishes? Younger children need tasks broken into smaller steps. (Actually, we *all* do, don't we? When I'm out of my element, learning a new computer program, for example, I need tasks broken into small, manageable steps!)

Instead of telling your child to put the dishes in the dishwasher, you might start with handing her each plate as you scrape it and get her to put it into the proper place. Be sure to point out specifically what she is doing correctly: "See how nice and straight that one is and how it fits in the rungs right beside the other one." Once she can do that, you can add another step and have her rinse or scrape the plate and then put it into the dishwasher.

Often, it is easier to teach tasks if we start from the end and work toward the beginning. Eventually, she'll be taking the plate from the table, scraping, rinsing, and then putting it into the dishwasher. Making chores a fun thing you can do together sets a cooperative and playful mood, and invites the child to help out, rather than ordering her to do so. Usually, the best time to start training children is when we just want to get them out of the way for efficiency sake – like when they're crawling into the dishwasher!

Some tasks can be very difficult to master and children may feel very frustrated or even fearful of learning them. Remember that acknowledging feelings and the difficulty of a new task can be very encouraging. Often *we need encouragement the most when we believe we* can't *do something.*

After learning about encouragement, one couple took their children skiing. They both came back and reported to the group how thrilled they were with their experience. Their story reflects their empathic listening skills as well as their use of encouragement. It is a wonderful example of helping children *move from can't to can.* Here is their story, broken into the steps that demonstrate the skills they used.

1. ***Start with where the child is at and acknowledge her present feelings***

   John crouched down to 7-year-old Brittany's level and said, "It can be very scary when we first learn to ski." Brittany nodded and John continued, "I wonder if you're afraid you'll get going too fast, lose control, and fall?" Then he paused and let Brittany talk. She simply nodded again, so he continued, "We're going to do this step by step, and I'll show you how you can control your speed, okay?" Again she nodded.

2. ***Break the task into manageable steps***

   "Don't worry about skiing to the bottom right now," said John. "We'll point our skis across the hill so we aren't going down very much at all. Notice that if you point your skis across the hill you don't go very fast." John demonstrated. "And if I turn my skis uphill, I stop. How about if you try skiing from where you are to me? Turn your skis and point them right at me."

3. ***Notice what they are doing right and verbalize it***

   "There, now, you see? You're controlling your speed by pointing your skis across the hill. Notice how you've got more pressure on your right foot. That's it. See how you can stop by pointing them uphill? How did that feel to be able to stop?"

John and his wife were excited about using these skills, not only because they were able to help their child get over some fears and learn to ski, but also because *they were able to get involved with their child.* Before applying these skills, they had found themselves impatient and cranky on the ski hill, waiting for their reluctant child.

Expectations: the good, the bad, and the ugly

Expectations are very important. Expectations can be a guide, giving our life direction and meaning. On the other hand, expectations can be a measuring stick we use to beat ourselves up. "Why can't I ever… How come I never… What's the matter with me?" These are tapes that play again and again inside our head when we set unrealistic expectations for ourselves. Unrealistic expectations keep us feeling inadequate and frustrated. If other people force their expectations upon us, we might even abandon our true self in order to live in accordance with their demands – anything just to keep the "peace" and get them off our back! Expectations can destroy our relationships with others and leave us lonely and isolated. That's why I call expectations the good the bad and the ugly.

The good

Expectations can help us create what we want in our life. We tend to find what we expect to find. When we set out expecting to find value in our relationship, we create value. We can expect that our children will be honest and respectful. As we look for evidence to support that expectation, we bring those traits out in our children. However, if we expect that our children will lie to us and continually accuse them of lying, they learn to lie just to avoid our wrath.

Children need realistic and age-appropriate expectations to aspire to. They gain a sense of accomplishment from achieving them. Having no expectations of your child keeps him from developing and understanding his capabilities and sends him a message that his contributions are not important to your family. Children need to feel capable and significant and they need to explore their own abilities to develop a sense of personal power. If we are expecting children to accomplish tasks and acquire skills beyond their age ability, we set them up for failure and ourselves up for frustration. In her book *Your Child's Self-Esteem*, Dorothy Corkille Briggs tells us that *children rarely question our expectations – they question their adequacy.* That's when expectations turn "bad."

The bad

Children measure what they can do against our expectations. As parents, we often want to push our children on to the "next step" – to urge them to achieve the next level before we have truly celebrated and appreciated the current step they are taking.

For example, as soon as our child crawls, we may encourage or even push him to walk. Instead of taking time to rejoice and celebrate the crawling stage, we're anxious for him to reach the next stage. Our child can get the message that whatever he does isn't quite enough. He can also miss important developmental stages. There is a reason children crawl. They are developing important neuro-pathways that are essential for other learning tasks.

Many times parents push their child ahead of their developmental level. We put our child on top of the slide before he can climb the ladder. We expect him to control his emotions and follow our rules before he is capable of even recognizing that he *has* emotions. We want him to share his brand new truck before he has developed a sense of trust that when he gives his truck away it will be returned to him. Sharing is a complex concept. Many adults are not too keen on sharing, yet we expect our child to share. Expecting children to achieve developmental milestones before they are ready leaves them feeling frustrated and inadequate.

To avoid pushing your children too far ahead of their abilities, a good rule of thumb is to follow your child's lead. Give him time to experiment learning various tasks. Provide opportunities for him to learn, and facilitate that learning. Children learn about themselves, their abilities, and the world around them through play. So give them lots of play opportunities, but do not over-organize or dictate their play. Provide simple toys, and encourage play in all that they do, from climbing stairs to putting on socks. Celebrate what they can do right now, rather than pushing them to the next level.

If we expect children to be able to tie their shoes at three years old, we set them up for failure. Sometimes parents receive a lot of pressure from others. "My child was potty trained at 18 months!" And we think, what's wrong with *my* child? What's wrong with me? So we push our child to do something he is developmentally unprepared for. At the very least, we take a long time to potty train him. At the worst, we set up a pattern of rebellion or self-destructive thought and behavior. That's when expectations turn ugly.

The ugly

When we expect the people around us to act in a certain way in order to fulfill our needs, expectations turn ugly. If we pressure our child to act in certain ways because we need to prove our worth as parents, we will destroy our relationship with our child and make ourselves miserable. We nag, control, and manipulate them to fulfill *our* expectations. When they rebel against our pressure, and we expand our manipulative tactics, expectations become as ugly as they can get.

Children may get stuck in what Gordon Neufeld calls a "counter-will" mindset. This is sometimes mistakenly perceived as strong will, but in actuality these children have no will of their own. Their only will is to defy authority. Not all children will outwardly rebel, however. Sometimes the child denies his true self in order to live more peacefully, at least outwardly with his parents. He will change himself to win approval from the all-powerful people he lives with. Dorothy Corkille Briggs calls this the "tragedy of the lost self." When we force our expectations on our children, we destroy our relationship with them and rip apart their self esteem.

Think about your expectations. Ask yourself the following questions.
- What expectations do I have for myself and for my child?
- Are they realistic?
- Where did I get them?
- What purpose do they serve?
- Are they helpful in building a strong relationship with my child?
- Are my expectations the source of troubles in our relationship?
- Do they inspire or discourage me and/or my child?
- Check for expectations that meet your needs alone. For example,

do you expect your child to learn piano because it meets her need or yours?

- Weed out expectations you've followed blindly, but that have no meaning for you or your child.

We gain our sense of who we are through what we give

I sometimes hear parents complain, "I give and give and give with my kids. I change my life around just to suit them, and do you think I get one ounce of appreciation? Not an ounce – all they ever do is complain!"

Think about this scenario for a moment, and put yourself in the child's shoes. If your parent is giving-giving-giving, you, as the child, are taking-taking-taking. Now ask yourself, "How fulfilling is taking?" Taking is empty; giving is fulfilling. Remember that to have healthy self-esteem and to succeed in life, we must see ourselves as significant. It is giving that allows us to feel significant. It is in giving that we discover who we are. *Truly, we gain our sense of who we are through what we give, not through what we take.* So be sure not only to *allow* your children to give, but *insist* that they do. Tell them and show them that you *need* them, that their contribution to your home is absolutely essential.

§

FIVE-YEAR-OLD BRANDON wanted to make supper. Of course, he wanted to create his own dish, so his family had what came to be known as "Bread Crisp." He'd cut up slices of bread, melt butter, and drizzle it over the bread. Then he'd throw on a can of creamed corn and, with his mother's prompting, add a bit of cheese, stick it in the oven and voila – "Bread Crisp" for supper! The delight that radiated from Brandon added immensely to the flavor of that dish. Today, he still cooks, and he's good at it, too.

§

Many families no longer have Mom, Dad, and the kids all living under the same roof. Often this is regarded as a disadvantage when it comes to raising children. Kelly, however, found the advantage within the "disadvantage" and used it to strengthen her family.

§

A SINGLE PARENT for the past six years, Kelly had been working hard to keep up with the demands of living. There was no question about it, she absolutely needed her children's help, and they knew it. She simply couldn't keep up with the household chores, yard work, and repairs around the house without them.

One of the challenges Kelly faced was establishing a new home away from the home her children had grown up in. Because they traveled back and forth between their dad's place (the original "homestead") and her place, they still thought of their dad's place more as "home."

Last summer, however, Kelly and the kids renovated the yard and her 15- and 17-year-old boys took on a project: building a rock wall, complete with a pond and some very impressive stone steps. Kelly had looked forward to helping her boys – she thought it might be good therapy. (A friend had told her that building a rock wall had been marvelous therapy for him!) However, it took only one large boulder to convince her that if she kept on with it she would need therapy all right – physiotherapy!

It was a project Kelly couldn't do; she needed the boys to do it. The boys knew far more about building the wall than she did anyway. Their dad offered them all of the how-to guidance they needed, and they were completely in charge. It was during the building of that wall that Kelly felt the boys really "buy in" to their home.

§

Giving children projects and letting them take complete charge of them is a marvelous way for them to learn, and for you to make the statement, "You are important and essential in the running of this home."

Children need to feel capable, significant, and powerful. We can help our children experience all three of these things by giving them tasks that they can manage themselves and that make a notable contribution to our home. You may need to teach them some skills initially, and schedule check-in times to see how it's going. But once you put them in charge, leave them there. Be their guide if necessary, but do not overstep your boundaries. They need to be empowered and trusted to carry out the task. Of course that task will vary according to age and ability and previous training. Set up opportunities for them to succeed.

Summary

An excerpt from "Family Education," North American Society of Adlerian Psychology, summarizes encouragement as follows.

To be encouraging

1. Look for strengths.
2. Ensure successes. Divide up large tasks into smaller more manageable ones.
3. Provide opportunities for the child to contribute. Give real jobs.
4. Avoid regularly doing for the child what the child can do for him/herself.
5. Recognize effort and improvement. Avoid criticism.
6. Give feedback. Be specific.
7. Look for analyzing ability, critical thinking, and good judgment. Discover why a child answers the way s/he does. It may be incorrect but rarely illogical:
    a. How did you come up with this?
    b. What did you think I meant?
    c. When you did that, what did you think would happen?
    d. Did you learn anything new or surprising? What will you do next time?
8. Demonstrate learning from mistakes!

Encouragement is the art of giving the gift of courage – the courage to trust and believe in oneself, the courage to make mistakes and keep going, the courage to live life rather than sit on the sidelines, the courage to take risks and to believe in our capacity to meet life's challenges, the courage to withstand peer pressure and to make decisions that are right for us, and the courage to live a life of honesty and integrity.

Give your child the gift of courage in life. Set her free to make mistakes, to live life, to try new things. Help her to understand her strengths, talents, and abilities. Help her to listen to her inner voice and to trust it as her guide in life.

Imagine two boats drawn up to the shoreline. One bears the inscription, "Nothing ventured; nothing gained," the other, "Nothing ventured; nothing lost." These are, basically, the only two attitudes to choose from in life. Which boat do you want your child to choose? The first is the boat of encouragement – the second, the boat of discouragement. Do we want our children to live life fully, or do we want them to watch from the shore as it sails by?

These are the gifts of courage and these are the gifts we give our children when we follow the suggestions above and throughout this chapter. Encouragement in turn gives *us* the gift of truly knowing our children, of knowing how to become involved with them in their world right here and now.

Encouragement is the key that opens the door to being present with our children, and being present is the key that opens the door to our children's hearts.

7

The Way of Living Harmoniously with Others

Helping Kids To Get Along with Each Other & Live Together Peacefully

When parents opt for peace at any price, the price of peace gets higher and higher.

The sibling relationship provides the training ground for other relationships.

We live in an interactive world. Strong interpersonal and social skills are crucial to success in today's world, both in our work as well as in our personal lives and relationships.

It can be very disconcerting when our children have difficulty playing with other children and sometimes we may wonder if they will ever develop the skills they need to get along peacefully and happily with others. Our anxiety over this issue can create more problems for us and for our child. Remember that developing these skills takes time and patience.

The relationship that you have with your child is the most important factor in helping him to develop social skills. As you listen carefully to him, he will learn to listen to others. As you invite him to be involved in the problem-solving process, he will learn to solve his problems with others. As you encourage him to develop his talents and abilities, he will learn to use them in relationship to others. Never underestimate the role your relationship plays in your child's social development.

Some children take longer than others to develop their social skills. Do not be too hasty, therefore, to push him out the door to daycare. Young children who are shy about leaving your side should be encouraged to venture out in their own time. Dorothy Corkille Briggs tells us that, "Safety must come first before a child can venture forth to the new." Relish and enjoy a close relationship with your child, and, when he is ready, give him space and permission to make mistakes as he develops his social skills.

You can also create a safe place for learning social skills by setting up opportunities for your child to succeed in social situations. Invite a child over who is socially gifted and create a one-to-one scenario. Have toys available that invite cooperative play. Avoid TV, Nintendo, and Internet games.

Use listening and encouragement to help your child learn social skills. For example, if your six-year-old is having great difficulty learning to play with others, you might do the following.

- Acknowledge the difficulty and identify the emotions. "Learning to get along with others can be pretty tough. Looks like you want to play with Ian and Jared, but you're not sure how to join in. Maybe you're feeling a little shy." Stop and listen to your child's response. Just talking about it may help. He may not say anything, however, so you can continue.

- "Sometimes it helps just to watch how they're playing. They've got a big dump truck and a grader. I see some other machinery over there that's not in use. Maybe they need some help." Again, wait and listen. Invite him to talk about how the other toys could help out with Ian and Jared's project. He may jump in at this point without discussing anything. If so, let him go! It's what we want. If he's still hesitating, encourage him to see himself using the front end loader. "Do you think maybe that loader over there would be helpful? Maybe if you go over and start using it, they'll ask you to join them, or they'll come and join you. You could even ask if you could join them."

- If your child is still reluctant to join, be patient. Continue to provide one-to-one play experiences. Keep the communication lines open so that your child can express his feelings.
- When your child is successful at joining in the play, you can review the process later. Ask him to tell you how he managed to do it.

Remember that children all have different personalities and preferences. Some children may be happy with only one friend, and others may seek many. Be careful not to project your own anxieties and preferences onto your children.

When my son started high school, I'd ask him about his day. Who'd he have lunch with? Did he find his cousin at lunchtime? When he told me he ate lunch by himself, I was very concerned. When I was 13, to be seen eating lunch by myself was an announcement to the world that I had no friends. I was a loser, a loner. Jason saw my distress and said, "It's okay, Mom. I *like* eating lunch by myself. It's so interesting just to watch other kids."

You can help your child learn to play with friends and with her siblings, provided you find age-appropriate activities for both. The sibling relationship provides a testing ground for our children's social skills. Give them space to experiment, but set some guidelines so that all of your children feel safe.

Sibling rivalry – the training ground for relationships

There are special circumstances that affect the sibling relationship, and that relationship has tremendous impact on our child's development. The remainder of this chapter is devoted to ideas and tools you can use to encourage healthy sibling interaction.

Cooling the fires of sibling rivalry

Imagine that your partner or spouse comes home one day, slips an arm around you, and says, "Honey, I love you so much, I'm going to bring home another partner just like you!" In their book *Siblings without Rivalry*, Adele Faber and Elaine Mazlish use that analogy to help parents understand the emotional turmoil children can go through when their new baby brother or sister joins their home. It helps parents to empathize with their child when he is grappling with jealousy and other emotions toward his sibling.

Put yourself in your child's shoes by playing along with this new partner scenario and imagine the situations that really tip off your jealousy: the new partner gets your old bed; the new partner gets some very special intimate attention; the new partner gets clothes you've already outgrown (even if they were your favorites and you don't want to let go); the new partner gets the relatives' attention, and so on.

Putting yourself in your child's shoes will help you know what to do to ease the tension. Imagine you've gone to your spouse to complain about the new arrival. You want him to take her back. Will it help your situation if he lectures you, appeals to your logic, or dismisses your request as ridiculous? Of course not! *You need to know he understands!* This is the first step in helping your child deal with antagonistic feelings toward a sibling.

- Simply listen and let your child know you understand.
- Clarify and identify his feelings.
- Then look at any unmet needs.

Perhaps your child is missing intimate contact with you. Discuss ways your child can have that need met. Your conversation might go something like this.

§

MOM IS NURSING the new baby. Three-year-old Jeremy comes around the corner and bursts into tears: "I hate the baby! Take her back!"

"You really don't like having the baby around." *Mom shows Jeremy she heard him.*

"Take her back, Mommy." Jeremy cries.

"I bet you feel a little jealous of Alisha. It's really hard for you to share my attention with her." *Mom gives Jeremy's emotion a name.* Jeremy is struggling to get up into Mom's lap. "I wonder if you miss the time you and I spent together, just you and me." *Mom guesses Jeremy's need.*

"Y-e-e-s-s-s-s-s!" sobs Jeremy.

"You know, honey, I miss it, too. Why don't you get one of your puzzles out and we can do it together just as soon as I put Alisha in her crib?" *Mom helps Jeremy to meet his need.*

"Okay," says Jeremy slipping off Mom's lap and running for his puzzle.

§

When Mom puts Alisha into her crib, it is imperative that she spend quality time with Jeremy. It doesn't need to be lots of time, but she and Jeremy need to connect – and stay connected.

Giving one-to-one attention to each child is a great way to help children release pent-up feelings that lead to aggressive behavior with their siblings. It also helps prevent those feelings from building up.

You can use this time to help your child gain skills to deal with his sibling situation. Instead of rushing in to "fix" rivalry situations when they occur, recognize that every relationship presents opportunities for learning. *Helping your child figure out how to deal with his sibling gives him valuable real-life skills.*

Here's an example of how a father coaches his son to handle his own situation.

§

"I HATE ANDREW, DAD," complains Ben, "he's so mean."

"I notice you have a tough time dealing with him some times." *Dad empathizes, but doesn't agree with Ben's description of his brother.*

"He always calls me a dork face! He's such a jerk!"

"Sounds like that really hurts your feelings." *Dad empathizes again and refrains from pointing out that Ben is also calling Andrew names. Pointing that out would only lead to a blaming, let's-talk-about-who's-really-wrong-here scenario. Dad's task here is to help Ben find ways he can deal with his brother, or with anyone else who calls him names. Dad needs to help Ben see that he has the power to let others get to him or not.* "I notice you really let him press your buttons."

"I don't let him! He just does," protests Ben.

"I wonder what would happen if you didn't react when he calls you dork face." *Gently, Dad helps Ben see how he gives his power away to his brother.*

"What do you mean?" Ben is curious now.

"Well, what if you just decided to leave the room and not give your brother any attention."

"That wouldn't work; he'd just call me something else."

"And if you ignored that as well?" prompted Dad.

"He'd get me some way," declares Ben.

"Ben, do you want your bother to have power over you?"

"Of course not!"

"Well, I hear you arguing for your brother now, telling me he has power over you."

"He's bigger than me, Dad, he does."

"Is that what you tell yourself, Ben – that your brother has power over you?" Ben is silent a moment.

"Ben, power isn't about control over someone else. It's about control over our own thoughts and actions. Andrew can't control you unless you let him. He can't 'get to you' unless you let him. You let him get to you by telling yourself he has power over you. Would you like to start telling yourself something different? Something that would give you power?" *Dad helps Ben develop a specific strategy to deal with his brother's name calling.*

"Like what?"

"What could you tell yourself that would keep you from hooking into your brother's name calling? Could you tell yourself it doesn't bother you and just walk away?"

"But it does bother me!"

"It bothers you because you let it, and only because you let it," insists Dad. "If you want to change that, you have to change the way you think. You have control over that. No one else is inside your mind telling you how to think."

"Ah!" the light goes on for Andrew. "Maybe I'll just tell myself I'm in charge and act like that, and he won't be able to get to me!"

Dad smiles. "Let me know how it goes."

§

Your first conversation with your child about power may not run so smoothly. I have found it takes time, patience, and persistence in pointing out where my child has power in his life and encouraging him to act on it. The point is that *when you speak with your child about handling the rivalry situation you empower him to handle it himself.* When parents step between two siblings, it usually only generates more hostility.

Next time your kids fight, stay clear, unless, of course, someone is really getting hurt. Later, in one-to-one time, you can empathize, discover your child's needs, and help him to meet them.

Don't play the rescuer

If you find yourself always rescuing one child from the other, you may be setting up a triangle that entrenches you in the role of the rescuer and your children as the victim and the persecutor.

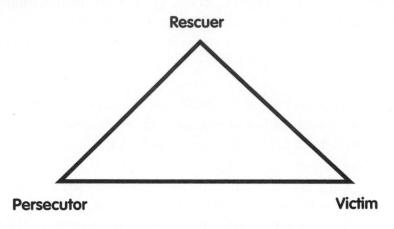

How many times have you seen "the victim" come wailing to Daddy, seen Daddy jump to punish the persecutor, and seen the victim smile ever so quietly? It's a classic scene, and parents get caught in it all the time. Beware of falling into this trap, for it ensures that the victim and the persecutor role will continue in your family.

Years ago when the boys were little, I saw the three-year-old chasing the one-year-old around the house. They were both laughing and giggling until the one-year-old did a face plant on the floor. Now, I saw him fall and knew that his brother was a good six feet behind him when he did so. Still, the three-year-old took one look at me as I came around the corner, threw his hands high in the air, and declared, "I didn't touch him!" I, of course, knew he hadn't, but his reaction made me take a step back and ask myself if I had habitually been treating him as the persecutor in the past.

One father complained that he had to help his young son because his older sister was always bossing him around. It had become his habit to step in and let the older girl know she was not to boss around her younger brother. I asked the father if he could foresee a time in his son's life when it would be handy for his son to be able to stick up for himself. Did he think that learning how to deal with a bossy older woman might be an asset?

"Of course," replied the father, and at that moment a light went on for him. "You mean, instead of trying to keep her from bossing him around I could help him learn how to handle himself?"

Yes! Siblings often provide us with opportunities to grow and learn how to handle the world outside our home.

Making a habit of rescuing can create both short- and long-term damage. In the immediate future, the punished child will likely seek revenge. Over the long term, we set our family up for the roles we play not only in our family, but throughout the rest of our lives.

Help children recognize the learning opportunity each relationship in their life presents. When we try to fix everything for them, we deny them the opportunity to learn and grow through that experience.

"But how can I stand back and watch my older child hit his little brother?" many parents will argue. It is a challenging situation for parents.

If you are worried that someone may get hurt, you can say, "Stop! It looks like you two are going to hurt each other. You need some time apart to cool down." Then, without blame or judgment, separate them.

If *both of them* insist that they are only play fighting, you can insist that they take their play fight somewhere else, or you can choose to leave the room if it bothers you. One mom told me she found it very effective to excuse herself from the room when the kids started fighting. As soon as the fight was over, she'd return and touch them gently on the arm, thanking them for taking care of the problem on their own.

Teach kids the difference between tattling & reporting

Tattling is when you come to tell me about something your brother is doing because you want to get him into trouble. Reporting is when you come to tell me your brother is in trouble and you think he needs my help.

Reporting is important if someone else is in danger, or if property is being destroyed. But if the main purpose in relating something to Mom or Dad is to get someone into trouble, it is tattling.

When you talk with your children, give some examples so that they understand.

- If Terry sneaks cookies without asking, and you tell me about it, ask yourself, are you telling me because *Terry is in trouble or might get hurt and needs my help*, or are you telling me because *you want Terry to get into trouble* with me? Since Terry is not in trouble, this would be tattling.

- If Terry is sitting on the floor in the shed opening the gasoline can, *Terry is in danger and it is very important that you report what he is doing to me.* In this case you would be telling me because Terry is in trouble and he needs help.

You can give some other examples, or have your children come up with their *own* examples that clarify the difference between tattling and reporting. Make it a game. What if Jeremy comes to tell me that Kate didn't wear her sweater on the playground at school? Would you be tattling or reporting? If Kate comes to tell me that Jeremy is using his father's chain saw, is that tattling or reporting? Some examples will be clearer than others. Help children see it is the *intention* that counts. Tell them you want them to solve their own problems, unless someone is in danger.

Tell your children that you will only listen to reporting from now on. Then do it! That's the hard part, of course, because we have a tendency to want to enforce all of our rules. So if one of our children reports that someone else has broken one of our rules, we think we should deal with it.

In such a situation, ask yourself what is most important in the big picture, in your family vision. Think about the impact your relationship with your own siblings has had on your self-esteem; on your memories of growing up. The sibling relationship is almost as influential in determining self-esteem as the parent-child relationship. *Fostering a cooperative relationship among your children is more important, in almost all cases, than correcting the "wrong" that is reported.*

When parents take action because of a tattletale, it can destroy relationships and everyone's peace of mind. It forms that unhealthy triangle, with Mom or Dad being the rescuer, the tattler being the "good guy," and the "persecuting" sibling being the "bad guy."

Understand that it is not your job to play M. Justice! In my first year of teaching, I believed it was my job to bring justice to every injustice on the playground. Every time a child came to me saying, "Teacher, Johnny called me an airhead!" I'd sympathize and say, "Let's go talk to Johnny together." Out to the playground we'd go, where I'd slip an arm around poor little Kathy and insist that Johnny apologize to her "right now." Of course, Johnny would "apologize" and I'd be on my way back into the school when another child would come up with a similar complaint. And then another, and another, and another. I spent my entire lunch and recess time "solving" disputes on the playground. Then I read an article that helped me to see how I was actually *creating* the never-ending steam of complainants. Immediately, I stopped running to set everything right and started to simply listen to the kids. Sometimes I'd help them think through the situation and come up with their own solution. Sometimes simply hearing their feelings was enough. And sometimes I'd just tell them I wouldn't listen to tattling.

> Fostering a cooperative relationship among your children is more important, in almost all cases, than correcting the "wrong" that is reported.

Avoid comparisons

Think back to the new spouse or partner illustration and imagine typical scenarios that would aggravate your jealousy. What if your partner decided to "motivate" you to become a better cook or gardener, by constantly comparing your skills to those of the new partner? Our children are no less affected when we use comparisons to motivate *them*.

Some parents think they will motivate their child to do better if they compare him to Brother Jake, or Cousin Richard. This does nothing but create resentment. We are only motivated when we compare ourselves to someone *we* want to be like. Your children must choose their own mentor!

Fair doesn't mean equal

Sometimes in our attempts to treat our children with unquestionable equality, we can keep children in competition with each other. If Sara complains that Tara received more Cheerios than she did, and we then count the Cheerios to even them up, we will spend much of our life counting Cheerios, and everything else. It will actually escalate the sibling rivalry as the children become pre-occupied with making sure everything is "even."

Instead of arguing about how many Cheerios Sara has, or struggling to make it "even," we can simply focus on meeting Sara's need. "Oh, Sara, do you want more Cheerios?" Then give her some. "Is that enough?"

Still, children complain, "It's not fair!" We can respond best to this by teaching children that *fair doesn't mean equal*. Fair means each person gets what they need. Sometimes Jayme will need to spend some extra time with Dad because she needs help looking after her horse. If sister Kerrie complains and demands Dad's attention *now*, Dad can explain that he'd like to spend time with Kerrie, too, but right now Jayme needs his full attention. He can then set a time to spend just with Kerrie.

Fear & threats don't really "keep the peace"

Avoid using fear and threats to "keep the peace." Remember that emotions drive behavior and that, if we prevent the expression of frustration and other volatile emotions, our kids may not fight when we're around, but the environment when we're not there may become dangerously hostile and out-of-control, or our children may turn their anger inward on themselves. Using fear to stop our children from fighting also keeps us playing "the heavy" and prevents us from connecting in meaningful ways with our children.

Helping children resolve conflicts on their own

If children are continually fighting and arguing and everyone seems miserable, the first step may be to call the children together *when both of them are calm* and to let them know that you want to discuss some solutions and alternatives to the arguing.

When they are together, you can follow the same problem-solving formula we've already outlined, except each of the children will state the problem from their point of view. Here's the process.

- Each child states the problem from his or her perspective.
- If you are the mediator, listen empathetically and reflect back the concerns of each child.
- Once the problems have been clearly stated, the secret is to focus on solutions.
- Brainstorm possible solutions with your children. You may want to do this verbally or write suggestions down.
- Select and agree upon a solution to try.
- Set a time to check in.

Sometimes it isn't necessary to go through so many steps. Sometimes it's okay to simply tell your children that until they come up with a solution they both agree upon, no one will play with the toy, or whatever. You might want to sit them down together in one room and tell them they can get up when they've both agreed the problem is resolved. It is amazing how creative they can be. They will come up with solutions you would never have imagined in a million years! And they may suggest agreements *you* would never have agreed to, but that doesn't matter. After all, they are the only ones who have to live with it.

Once kids have some problem-solving skills, leave them alone! It's our duty to give them some tools. However, if we find ourselves going over and over these "tools" every time the kids fight, we'll find them fighting a lot. We are still feeding their fights with our attention.

Teach children how to cooperate
& get what they want

Teaching children how they can get what they want *and* get along with others can ward off many arguments and foster cooperation in your home.

§

SHARON WAS EXASPERATED. It seemed to her a never-ending battle to keep her daughter and son from fighting. Who was it that told her that the closer siblings are in age, the more intense the relationship? Boy, were they ever bang on! Kyle was nearly three-and-a-half and Taylor just turned two. As soon as one of them had a toy, the other one wanted it. Sharon reminded herself to step back and observe the dynamics, and suddenly a stroke of genius hit her. What if she was able to teach her kids to get what they wanted without fighting?

"Wait a minute," Sharon called out unexpectedly, interrupting her children in mid-struggle. (Kyle was desperately trying to wrench a toy out of screaming Taylor's grip.) "Kyle, I bet there's a better way to get what you want." Kyle looked at her curiously. "Think about it, Kyle." Sharon knelt down beside him and tapped one long index finger to her temple. "Think, Kyle, think."

Then she got a piece of paper. "Look, Kyle, let's think about some ways you can get what you want without struggling." Both her children watched her as she wrote down, "How to Get What I Want." They couldn't read the words, but they were impressed that she was writing this down for them. Kyle was really interested now. Even Taylor was watching her mother closely.

"What's one way to get something? What do you do when you want something?"

"Ask for it?" guessed Kyle.

"Right! Let's write that down. Number 1. Ask nicely," Sharon spoke the words as she wrote them.

"Won't work," pouted Kyle.

"That's okay," Sharon reassured him. "There are other ways. What else?"

"Don't know," said Kyle.

"How about trading," Sharon prompted him. "You know, lots of times Taylor would be happy if you simply traded – give her another toy for the toy she has. Do you think that might work?"

"Maybe," said Kyle.

"Let's write it down, too," said Sharon, "Number 2: Trade. What else do we do sometimes, Kyle? When we're building a tower with our blocks, I put a block on, then you put a block on, then it's my…"

"Turn," said Kyle with a big smile. "Take turns."

"Right! Let's write it down. Number 3, take turns. We could even get the timer out and you could set it. When the bell rings, it will be your turn. Now Kyle, if that doesn't work, there's one more thing you could try. You know how sometimes you snuggle under the blanket and Mommy's cold too? Sometimes you share with me. Do you think sometimes you could share with Taylor?"

"Maybe," said Kyle.

"Let's write it down," suggested Sharon, "Number 4, share. So here they are, Kyle:

1. Ask nicely
2. Trade
3. Take turns
4. Share

"Let's keep it right here on our fridge to remind us next time you want something, here are some things you can try to get it."

That paper stayed on the fridge for a long time and Kyle became the best little negotiator for miles around. Sure, he and Taylor still had their struggles, but at least now he knew there were other ways to get what he wanted. The visual reminder of the list on the fridge helped, too.

§

A word about sharing. Sharing is a developmental skill. Dorothy Corkille Briggs cautions us that "owning comes before sharing. Only 50 percent of three-year-olds can share – and then only briefly."

A timer that children can see and set themselves can work wonders to help them to learn to take their turn. It can also help parents.

§

JOAN OFTEN FELT there just wasn't enough time to do things with her children. They wanted her to play with them, and even though Joan wanted to do just that, there always seemed to be something else demanding her attention. Joan did notice, however, that if she didn't go and play when they asked, it wasn't long before they would get her attention anyway. Either she'd be in their rooms solving another dispute, or they'd be with her, hanging on to her pant legs. Playing with them would have been a lot more fun.

Then, one day, a friend told Joan about the timer she used. When her kids asked her to play, she'd say, "Okay, but I can only play for ten minutes and then I have to get supper ready." They'd all set the timer and away they'd go. Having established this agreement, she felt she could really get into playing with her children. It was like taking a ten-minute break from her work. If she couldn't play right then and there, she'd set the timer for ten minutes later and her kids were happy.

Joan introduced the timer with her kids and found they all really liked it. The kids seemed happier when they could see the time ticking by, and Joan felt better about knowing she was spending quality time with her children. Sometimes they used the timer to count down the time before dinnertime, or until bedtime. The timer became the authority and there were fewer arguments with Mom and Dad. They even used the timer to set goals. Joan was actually able to teach her children to sit and draw on their own for longer and longer lengths of time. Joan was amazed at how much difference one little timer could make.

§

Activities & games that build cooperation in the home

You can save a lot of time arguing with your child by proactively establishing an environment of trust and cooperation. Take time to participate in activities with your children that require and encourage cooperation. If possible, start with activities your child is already engaged in, such as Lego building, Tinkertoys, or, as they get older, listening to music or taking part in sports activities. Let your child take the lead, if possible – join them in *their* game. Don't worry if you're not as good at it as your child is – it will do them wonders to *teach* you! Together, you'll be able to generate lots of ideas for more projects. Here are a few to get you started.

- Make decorations for special occasions.
- Tell cooperative stories on tape. Start with one, two, or three words; then pass the story to the next person, who adds the agreed-upon one, two, or three words, and so on.
- Create "secret pals" for Christmas and other occasions. Here everyone draws a name from a hat and it is their job to do nice things for that person without getting "caught." One friend of mine made it a habit every New Year's to have a candlelight celebration of each other's attributes. If you drew someone's name, you needed to come up with three things you really liked about that person and share them at the candlelight celebration. Mom and Dad were always included in this exercise.

- Color a personalized calendar for the year and give it to Gramma or Grampa.
- Plan and decorate your child's room together.
- Make forts, or stores, or houses, etc., from boxes and other scrap materials.
- Make musical instruments and have a family "jam session." Even the kids' guitars and homemade shakers can be lots of fun. We had many a "jam session" when my children were young and today they are still jamming together, although their instruments have gotten a little more expensive.
- Send a message to the North Pole via the tape recorder. Children love to hear their own voices, and learn to listen and take their turn. You can recount the year's highlights as well as tell Santa what your list is. These are wonderful journals and keepsakes as the kids get older.
- Look for opportunities to celebrate, and invite everyone to contribute.
- Take time before the family meal to express gratitude for the food you are sharing and for being together. This creates a positive environment. Gratitude is very powerful.
- Create a large mural for your wall, or create a wall chart to measure increasing heights.
- Add your own ideas.

Summary

Helping children learn to get along lays the foundation for the interpersonal skills that last a lifetime. It takes time and patience to develop these skills, however. They will learn many of these skills through their relationship with you. Nurture your relationship, first and foremost. Then, provide opportunities for your children to learn and practice these skills with others. Recognize the important role sibling relationships plays in developing social skills.

Attempting to keep the peace and settle children's fights often increases the amount of quarrelling between children. Remember that whatever we give our attention to will grow. If we give attention to our children each time they argue, they may learn to argue simply to get our attention.

Before you give your children's arguing any attention whatsoever, ask yourself, "Is this just normal bickering? If I leave them alone, what will happen? Can they resolve the dispute, or will it simply dissolve?" Often, we are too concerned that our children will get hurt if we don't step in. Take a step back for a moment and ask yourself, "Which is more important: preventing one child from hurting the other physically, or teaching children to get along as brothers and sisters?" And, if you have spent your time and energy trying to prevent every scrape and bruise from happening, ask, "Is it working, or are they still fighting anyway?" If it isn't working, step back from the scene of the crime and look honestly at what is happening. Are you setting up a pattern that is creating chaos and hurting relationships all around?

8

The Way of
Loving Discipline

Providing guidance in a context of love, respect, & responsibility

*Just because you've silenced someone
doesn't mean you've gained their consent.*

Discipline gives life to learning.
— BARBARA COLOROSO

*Some people regard discipline as a chore.
To me, it is a kind of order that sets me free to fly.*
— JULIE ANDREWS

Do you have the discipline to be a free spirit?
— GABRIELLE ROTH

"Don't sweat the small stuff."
— RICHARD CARLSON

❧

DISCIPLINE IS A WORD that used to make me cringe. Somehow it brought the rebel out in me.

Then one day a man said to me, "You know, in order to be free, you have to have discipline." I looked at him suspiciously. Was this another ploy to get me to buckle under, to do as he told me to? Was it another manipulative tactic that would exploit my power?

"I don't think so," I retorted, "How can that be?"

"Well, think about it for a minute. If you want to feel free and safe to drive to the other side of town, you have to have the discipline to follow the rules of the road. If you want to have the freedom that health and fitness bring you, you have to have the discipline to exercise and eat properly."

"Hmm, I guess I hadn't thought about it that way," I said, my idea of discipline beginning to shift.

I went home that night and thought about how much time and energy I had invested rebelling against the disciplinarians in my life, believing that if I could just unload the "disciplinarians," I'd be free. That night a new idea of discipline formed in my mind. I thought, "If I could discipline myself not to eat so much, and to exercise regularly, I'd be a lot happier." Up until then, I had confused discipline with punishment and had spent my life avoiding both – I wanted to be a "free spirit." That night I began to see that to be a truly "free spirit" I would need to discipline myself. *I started to see discipline as the key to obtaining what I want in my life. I started to see that true freedom emerges from discipline.*

❧

How can parents help children to grow up viewing discipline as a tool they can use to obtain what they want? One thing is clear: as long as children view discipline as punishment, it will not be something they seek for their own benefit.

Dictionaries provide a number of definitions for the word "discipline." "Punishment" is included in those definitions. Discipline is also defined as training of the mind or character. Confusion has resulted because many people believe that punishment is about training the mind or character. Effective discipline means helping children acquire self-discipline, through developing and strengthening the inner qualities that will help them to achieve their goals and to act responsibly in our families and communities. Punishment often provokes rebellion, resentment,

> I started to see discipline as the key to obtaining what I want in my life. I started to see that true freedom emerges from discipline.

and revenge, or sends kids into withdrawal and retreat. It is therefore necessary to make a clear distinction between punishment and discipline, as we shall refer to it here.

Understanding the difference between punishment & discipline

§

ONCE UPON A TIME there was a great land that was divided into two kingdoms: the Kingdom of Did and the Kingdom of Didn't. Each of the kings wanted the best for their kingdom, but they had different ideas about how to rule.

As it often is, their differences became most noticeable in times of strife. When a great drought fell over the land, both kingdoms were in crisis, and both kings moved to save their kingdom.

The King of Didn't sent a decree out to the villages with a strict warning that water rations were now in place and that the people could water their property only on certain days. Anyone caught watering on days other than their watering days would be punished. The king would be sending his men around to make sure that his law was enforced.

The King of Did sent a message to his people that there was trouble in the land and that he would require the help of all of the people to solve the problems they faced. He called for emergency meetings in each village. He started the meetings off by describing the problems they faced. "The water shortage has become severe. If we do not see rain very soon, we will all be out of water within two weeks time. What do you think we should do?"

The townspeople discussed the issue and agreed upon water rations much like the rations the King of Didn't had handed down.

In the weeks that followed, the King of Didn't sent his men around regularly to make sure the water rationing was enforced. The people of his kingdom wanted to make sure that no one would be punished, so they got together and appointed guards to watch for the king's men. When the guards saw them coming, they signaled the townspeople and the townspeople would stop watering. No one was ever caught, but no one obeyed the water rations either.

In the Kingdom of Did, the townspeople reminded one another of the water rationing when they saw that someone had forgotten. They encouraged one another to follow the guidelines they had developed to solve their problem.

As you can guess, the people in the Kingdom of Didn't soon ran out of water. The people in the Kingdom of Did were able to ration the water and make it through the drought.

§

This story helps to illustrate the difference between discipline and punishment. The townspeople of the Kingdom of Didn't were so concerned that they would be caught and punished, they ignored the danger of the drought. In the Kingdom of Did, the people were invited to help resolve the problem. They took ownership of the problem and stayed solution-focused. This is the heart of discipline.

Every time you need to discipline your child, ask yourself this very simple question: "Is this discipline aimed at helping my child find a solution to the problem at hand?" If your answer is no, it is not discipline, but punishment.

It's interesting that we use punishment because we want children to feel bad for what they've done – we want them to develop a conscience – we want to teach them right from wrong. Yet when I ask parents to remember back to a time when they were punished, few of them remember feeling bad about what they'd done and fewer still report a desire to make amends for their wrongdoing. Some can't even remember what they'd done! Often, people remember only their anger towards their punisher.

> In the Kingdom of Did, the people were invited to help resolve the problem. They took ownership of the problem and stayed solution-focused. This is the heart of discipline.

When we punish children, we back them into a corner. We don't give them space to feel bad for what they've done wrong. If we want children to be *response-able*, we must give them the space and skills to be *able* to *respond. Discipline encourages children to take responsibility for the issue at hand. It empowers them to be able to respond.*

In contrast, punishment aims to make a child feel so bad she will never repeat the "crime." It focuses on making the child "pay" for her misdeeds. Paying for misdeeds often involves demoralizing, humiliating, and stripping the child of power. Mistakes then become fearful events. The punished child may seek to avoid making mistakes by not taking any risks – "Nothing ventured, nothing lost." And so they live their lives

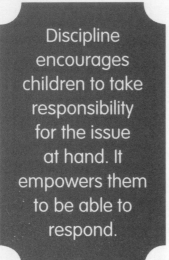

Discipline encourages children to take responsibility for the issue at hand. It empowers them to be able to respond.

in fear of the future, while mulling over the guilt and regret of the past.

The game of win-and-lose

Punishment ignites the game of "win-and-lose." I once heard a psychologist explain this clearly. She said that if, when we were small children, our parents played the game of win-and-lose with us, chances are good we always felt like we were the losers. (Parents learned that it was their duty, their role as a parent, to be the winners.) Silently, often subconsciously, we probably said to ourselves, "When I grow up, I am going to be the winner." Then, when we became parents, we made sure that we *were* the winners. The problem is that, if *we* have to be the winner, our *child* has to be the loser.

Let's stop playing the game of win-and-lose. It is as if we have been flipping the coin for generations – heads I win/tails you lose – and I will do everything in my power to make sure I win. This game gets us nowhere; both parties are stuck. Discipline is about changing the game and rolling the coin on its side and deciding that we can *both* win. The game doesn't have to be "me against you." Let's take a win-win attitude and approach to the situations that we face. Instead of me confronting you and needing to change your behavior, how about if we literally sit down side by side and put the problem, the issue, on the table. Let's use our problem-solving skills and look at this as an opportunity for both of us to grow.

Recently a friend of mine who is in his 60s said to me, "You know, I don't do conflict well. I never won against my mother and so all of my life I have run away from conflict. But this time, I decided not to run and for the first time I allowed myself to feel the emotions that are involved in conflict. And now I can see where conflict creates an opportunity to deepen my relationship – to create greater intimacy."

Much of traditional parenting has involved shutting down conflict and never allowing children to argue – turning off and hiding away uncomfortable emotions. This impacts us for the rest of our lives. It takes a lot of personal work to break through such patterns.

Recognize those times when you and your child are in conflict as an opportunity to deepen your relationship, as an opportunity to work together to roll the coin on its side and to actually get somewhere. *We can create the solution rather than react to the problem. Discipline opens up opportunities for growth; punishment closes them down.*

Punishment fuels the fires of resentment, rebellion, & revenge

Take a moment to think back to a time when you were punished. Imagine it as vividly as you can. What happened? Who was the punisher? How did you feel? Were you truly sorry for your actions, or were you too angry or upset at the punisher to be sorry? If you were punished because of something you did to your brother or sister, how did you feel about them after receiving your punishment? Did you spend your "punishment time" plotting revenge? Perhaps you turned that anger towards yourself? Did you want to make amends for what you'd done?

If Carly suddenly bops her younger brother Josh on the head with her toy, often, the parents' first reaction is to punish Carly so that she won't do it again. They may tell her she's a bad girl, or say, "Carly, go to your room and think about how mean you've been to your brother." They may spank her to *show her how it feels.* In her book *Your Child's Self-Esteem*, Dorothy Corkille Briggs talks about spanking this way: "Spanking does not teach inner conviction. It teaches fear, deviousness, lying and aggression. No matter how we slice it, spanking is a physical assault of a bigger person on a smaller person."

In their attempts to punish Carly, the parents are trying to make Carly feel so bad, she'll never do it again. But when Carly gets to her room, what do you think she's feeling? Chances are good she's angry and resentful and more jealous of her brother than ever (which is what may have provoked the attack in the first place). She may very well be thinking about the incident and how to gain revenge and not get caught next time! If her revenge thoughts are aimed at her brother, her parents' punishment tactics may have actually put their son at greater risk of being hurt.

Alternatively, Carly may go to her room and turn her thoughts on herself: "They're right. I *am* a bad, bad girl. I *never* do anything right." Carly may be confused about her own jealous emotions and hurt at being rejected by her parents. She may learn that the only way to survive is to deny her emotions and to focus all of her attention on pleasing her parents and avoiding their wrath.

While Carly's complacency may initially appear to make things easier for her parents, one needs to consider the long-term effects of this approach. The people I know who feared their parents' wrath and whose survival technique was to perceive and succumb to their parents' wishes have had to do much work just to be able to *feel* again. They have not trusted themselves or their own judgment. They have faced enormous fear in being honest with others about the way they feel.

In the incident with Carly and Josh, discipline would require that the parent stay solution-focused. Instead of reprimanding and punishing Carly (and giving her the attention), what if the parent scooped up Josh and gave Carly the opportunity to make amends?

"Oh, Josh, that really hurt. I guess Carly didn't know it would hurt that much." (Even if Carly has been downright "mean" lately, it still helps to call forth the inner qualities we want to see in our child.)

The parent can then invite Carly to make amends: "Carly! Quick, can you run and get your brother a cold cloth for his head?" If Carly doesn't want to help, stay focused on helping Josh (after all, he is the one who is hurt).

Now, maybe you're thinking that Carly is getting away with hitting Josh without any consequences. Carly's consequence is that she did not get the attention for hitting her brother, and in effect will realize that Josh has received more attention due to her actions.

At a later time, when Mom or Dad and Carly are having an intimate moment, they can talk about Carly's feelings and hopefully release the emotions that prompted the attack. Remember that to change behavior from the inside out we need to address the emotions that drive behavior. Discipline isn't always a one-step approach that instantly fixes the problem. It may be that parent and child will have to do some problem solving together, with the parent helping the child to find the discipline to carry out the agreed-upon solution. It may be that Carly really needs help dealing with her jealousy and bringing out her love for her brother. Remember that discipline is not about paying for the crime, but about developing the strength of character to take responsibility and make amends.

Punishment teaches kids to avoid being punished

"How to cover one's butt and not get caught" is the main lesson we teach kids when we use punishment. Barbara Coloroso illustrated this point very well in a story she told, during one of her presentations, about a young child who wanted to cross the road.

The child stood at the top of his driveway and, rather than looking both ways to see if there were cars coming, twisted and turned his body to see if his mother was watching. Deciding that the "coast was clear" (i.e., that Mom was nowhere to be seen) the child slapped a hand on each buttock and raced across the road. He was so busy making sure he didn't get caught that he didn't even think about watching for cars. Fear of punishment can actually put our kids in danger.

Ask yourself this: *"If your child is really in trouble and needs help, do you want her to come to you, or do you want her to hide from you?"* Punishment teaches her to hide from you. Punishment teaches her to sneak around. Punishment is often the root cause of lying.

§

WHEN SHERRY'S BOYS were three and five years old, she saw them climbing on some bins in their orchard. The boys knew they weren't supposed to be climbing on the bins, but when Sherry confronted them with it, they lied to her.

She said, "There is no point in lying to me, boys, I saw you. What concerns me far more than you climbing on the bins, is that you lied to me. Lying is not what I want in our relationship. And I think that if you have to lie, maybe it is because you are afraid I'll punish you. Is that why you lied?"

Their heads bobbed in unison. "Well," she said, "then we have two problems. First, you have to know that the reason I don't want you climbing on the bins is because you might hurt yourself. Those bins could fall off and you could really be hurt. The second problem is the lying. It's important to me that you know that I don't want to hurt you or punish you. It's important to me that we can be honest. I won't punish you, but I want to find a way to help you get what you need without climbing on the bins. What made you want to climb up there?"

"Cause it's fun."

"So you like climbing?"

"Yeah – there's nothing else to do."

"You were feeling a bit bored, were you?"

"Uh-huh."

"Well, maybe we can find somewhere safer where you can climb. If the bin falls on top of you, you could really get hurt."

They talked and negotiated and finally agreed on some trees the boys could climb. Eventually, they helped their dad build a tree house.

Since then, Sherry has reminded her kids repeatedly that she doesn't want them ever to feel they have to lie to her, or sneak around. She wants them to know she's on their side, helping them to get their needs met in responsible ways. She wants them to know they can come to her if they're in trouble, rather than avoid her for fear of being in more trouble.

§

Understanding the difference between discipline and punishment, and choosing discipline, will strengthen and support your relationship with your child. Remember that, ultimately, the only real authority you have with your child is that which she is willing to give you. The strength and health of your relationship together will determine her willingness to give you that authority. The following is a summary of the differences between discipline and punishment.

Discipline gives life to learning

Discipline
1. Is always solution-focused.
2. Shows kids specifically what they have done wrong, or states the problem clearly.
3. Gives kids ownership of the problem and encourages them to be responsible.
4. Leaves their dignity intact and is always respectful.
5. Never threatens withdrawal of parental love.

Punishment fuels the fires of resentment, anger, & revenge or forces retreat & withdrawal

Punishment
1. Is reactionary.
2. Does something *to* the child.
3. It is adult oriented and suits the parent's needs.
4. Teaches kids to avoid punishment.
5. Is only "effective" as long as the fear of punishment is present.
6. Does not invite the child's participation in solving problems.
7. Perpetuates the game of win-and-lose.

Natural and logical consequences

Helping children learn to deal with the consequences of their actions can be an effective way to teach them self-discipline. Whenever we allow or encourage children to face the consequences of their decisions and actions, we are helping them to build confidence in their ability to solve problems and to interact effectively in the world.

Sometimes all we need to do is get out of the way and allow the *natural consequence* to take place. Natural consequences are those consequences children encounter without interference from an adult. If a child doesn't eat the food provided for her, she is likely to become hungry later. Sometimes parents let their child know there will be a consequence, such as going hungry if the child refuses to eat her lunch, but then can't stand the whining and give in and feed her – exactly what she wants. (Of course, we make sure we hand out our standard "I told you so" lecture as we're making her something to eat!) As a result, she does not experience the natural consequence of hunger, because we've intervened. How often has a parent insisted that a child wear a coat (resulting in a power struggle), rather than allow the child to experience being cold and to make the decision to reach for her coat herself? These are ways parents stand in the way of children learning through natural consequences. We make ourselves the "police" and set ourselves up as adversaries, rather than allow children to learn the ways of the world.

Of course, if serious harm threatens our child, we need to step in. We don't allow our children to experience the "natural consequence" of getting hit by a car. However, parents often take it upon themselves to prevent their child from making mistakes and end up denying them the valuable opportunity of learning from the experience.

Sometimes natural consequences are either inappropriate or are insufficient to help children learn the important lessons of accountability and responsibility. That is when we need to implement consequences which will hold children accountable for their actions and decisions. These are called *logical consequences*.

Logical consequences are not meant to be a quick fix. Sometimes parents want a consequence for their child's misbehavior that will magically "fix" it. "When my child writes on the wall/throws a temper tantrum/yells at me…what can I do? What is the consequence?" What the parent often means with those questions is, "What can I do to ensure she will never do that again? How can I 'fix' her?"

Beware of focusing too intently on "treating" or "fixing" the misbehavior with consequences. Years ago, I heard Dr. Gordon Neufeld say something that has had a profound impact on my attitude toward applying logical consequences in the discipline process. "The only true authority we have with our children," he said, "is that which they are willing to give us." Neufeld explains that "the authority of the parent is a function of the child's attachment to the parent." We do not want to damage the attachment relationship we have with our child. Many times, we are so concerned with treating the misbehavior and with doling out consequences, that we forget that building a strong and healthy relationship with our child is the number one issue.

You can maintain a healthy relationship with your child by viewing logical consequences as a way to support her in making amends in the situation at hand. View them as strategies you (or you and your child) design to help your child meet the needs of the situation. Firmly and kindly help her to take ownership of the problem.

The characteristics of logical consequences

When developing logical consequences, remember that they must always be *respectful, realistic, reasonable,* and *related* to the incident. It also helps if the consequence can be *revealed* ahead of time and the child knows what to expect as a result of their decision not to comply with agreements. Let's look at each one of these characteristics individually.

- *Respectful:* Consequences should never demean or humiliate the child. Always address the child with dignity and respect.
- *Realistic:* Make sure both you and your child can live with the consequence. Taking away *all* of his toys and leaving him with nothing to play with may drive both of you crazy in very short order. Grounding your teen for a month may make that month the longest in history – for both you and your teen. It's important

to take action and to follow through with any consequence set, so don't tell her she can't go to Grandma's if there is *no* alternative!

- *Reasonable:* If your child has tracked mud onto a clean floor, having her clean the entire floor and the bathroom as well is not reasonable. It is reasonable to expect her to clean up the mud.
- *Related:* Remember to hold the child responsible for making amends and finding a solution. If you do, the consequence, of necessity, will be related. Understand that the child has been doing the best he can to get his needs met and your job is to help him find another appropriate way to meet his needs. The consequences of having used his brother for a punching bag may include not only making amends with his brother, but finding an acceptable punching bag to deter future squabbles.
- *Revealed:* Whenever possible, reveal consequences ahead of time. For example, your child understands that "forgetting" to stay on the sidewalk with her bike will result in having her bike put away for the next two days. Note that the length of time a consequence lasts varies according to the misbehavior and to the age of the child. Young children who have no concept of today and tomorrow need immediate consequences that shouldn't last long. For example, a three-year-old may have to give up her toy for the rest of the morning, while a teenager could lose privileges for two or three weeks.

How we implement logical consequences is more important than what the consequences are. It is our attitude, tone of voice, body language, and intent that determines whether a given consequence is really a logical consequence or has become a punishment.

Ask yourself if you are really saying, "I told you so… You deserve it… Suffer the consequences, kid… It serves you right… Ha, ha-caught you!" Or are you saying, "Gee, I'm sorry, but this is what happens now. I know it isn't pleasant, but it is necessary to set things right."

Intention is *so* important to discipline. It is easy for our intention to shift from support to condemnation. Consequences intended to discipline turn to punishment when we shift our intention from helping kids to make amends, find solutions, and meet their needs, to making them feel *so* bad they won't do it again. Always be respectful and remember that in the overall picture, strengthening your relationship is far more important than focusing on correcting, or ending, specific deeds of misbehavior.

§

WHEN JEFF WAS about 11, he got into the habit of losing his temper and pounding his brother on the shoulder – and he seemed to be losing his temper more and more frequently. One night at the dinner table, Jeff hauled off and slugged his brother.

"That's it!" his mother, Joanne, declared. "Jeff, if you can't sit at the table without hitting your brother, you'll have to leave."

Jeff pushed his chair back angrily and stomped toward the stairs.

"And, Jeff," Joanne called after him…

"I know, I know," Jeff snarled, and then added mockingly, "I can return when I've decided to act differently."

That mockery pushed Joanne's button instantly and she threw after him, "That's right – and if that time doesn't come before supper's over, you can just forget about eating tonight!" As soon as she said it, Joanne knew she had gone one step too far, for Jeff's mockery had both hurt her and challenged her. Her intention had shifted from discipline to

> **How** we implement logical consequences is more important than what the consequences are. It is our attitude, tone of voice, body language, and intent that determines whether a given consequence is really a logical consequence or has become a punishment.

revenge. She knew that the one thing she should not take away from Jeff was food – because ever since he was a baby, he was always grumpy and unreasonable if he was hungry.

Joanne realized that she had shifted to punishment mode, and so she gave herself time to cool down. She remembered that if they were really going to stop the hitting, *Jeff* would have to see how it would help *him* to get his temper under control. She also knew that if she went to his room and talked about how he must stop hitting his brother, Jeff would accuse her of sticking up for him. So, with the clear intention of helping Jeff to see how this hitting was hurtful and potentially dangerous to him, she went down to talk.

"Jeff, can I come in?"

Jeff grunted. Joanne interpreted the grunt to mean yes, so she opened the door gently. Jeff was sitting on the bed. Joanne went and sat beside him. "Jeff, I have some concerns about the punching and hitting you've been doing lately." Joanne paused while Jeff grunted again. "I just don't see it helping you in life. In fact, I can see it doing some real harm."

"Like what?" Jeff sounded a bit sarcastic, but Joanne held her intention to help him see how this hitting was hurtful to himself, as well as to others, and she managed not to react. Besides, underneath the surly tone, she did think he was curious.

"Well first, I see it doing some real harm to your relationship with your brother – you and he have always had lots of fun and been best friends, and I don't see either of you being very happy these days, or playing together like you used to do."

They both remained silent for a moment. Jeff shifted uneasily on his bed. "And," said Joanne, "I'm concerned that if you don't get a handle on your temper, you're going to slug the wrong guy someday and you might really get hurt. Someday you may end up in a bar somewhere with a knife in your back."

"Oh, Mom!" Jeff exploded, horrified. "Don't say that!"

"Well, think about it, Jeff. *When* are you going to learn to control your temper and stop slugging people? It's become a bad habit and every time you lash out and hit somebody, you just reinforce it. When are you going to stop?"

"Well it's just that – just – just that… I get so frustrated, I just want to hit somebody," Jeff's voice was strained and Joanne knew he was holding back tears.

"So punching helps you release your frustrations?" asked Joanne.

"Yeah, kind of."

"Well, punching your brother doesn't work. How about we get you something you can punch. Do you think that would help?"

"Yeah, I guess so, but what can we get?"

"How about a punching bag?"

"Well, as long as it's not like that punching bag you got us when we were little! That Fred Flintstone thing sucked – and it didn't last very long."

Joanne resisted the temptation to "correct" his language, and stuck to the issue. Remembering those punching bags made her laugh, and before they knew it they were both laughing. "No, I guess they didn't stand a chance with you and your brother. This time we'll get a real punching bag – gloves and all!"

"Really?" Jeff lit up. "Where will we put it?"

"Oh, we'll find a spot – maybe in the shed… But Jeff, you have to promise that you'll punch *it* – and not your brother – from now on."

Jeff promised and they both went upstairs to finish supper. Afterwards, they had a great evening checking the papers and flyers for punching bags.

The punching stopped right away, even though it took weeks to actually get the bag and mount it. Obviously, the talk was enough to help Jeff release some frustration and to decide that it was important to him to control his temper.

Once they put the bag up, Joanne would hear him pummeling it steadily. The whole house shook, but she didn't care. "At least he's not hitting his brother," she'd tell herself, "and he's got his temper under control!"

§

Notice how Joanne's intention was so important? She wanted to help Jeff see the benefits of controlling his temper. She held her intention to find a solution that worked foremost in her mind. There was no need to revert to the "consequence" of Jeff missing his supper. Joanne recognized that she had dealt out that consequence in a state of anger and seeking revenge. Keeping herself calm, Joanne stayed onside with her son, accepted his emotions, and maintained the position of supporting him in resolving the issue. She was respectful of Jeff, while letting him know clearly her concerns and limits.

When you are disciplining your child, stay focused on how to help him resolve the issue and make things better for everyone, especially for himself. Try asking your child quietly, "How is that behavior helping you? You don't have to tell me the answer, just go inside and ask yourself how your actions are helping you." Then back off. It's important the question is asked without blame and with the intent to help the child.

Once the emotion driving their behavior has been released, children often feel better when they've been able to make amends. Think of disciplining as a way of helping your child to meet his needs appropriately, and get the idea out of your head that your job is to make him feel bad, or to make him "suffer the consequences."

"Suffer the consequences" is a phrase that belongs only to the realm of punishment. Parents often ask, "But what if they *enjoy* the consequence? What if he *likes* cleaning the crayon drawings off the wall? What if he has a good time with the sponge and the water" I say great! Then we can teach them that if they make a mistake, cleaning it up doesn't have to be misery. "But won't they keep writing on the wall so they can get soapy and wet?" I reply, "Don't you have any other walls that need cleaning?" I don't know about you, but I *always* have walls that could use a good scrub and the amazing thing is, when my kids were young, the places the walls needed cleaning just happened to be within their reach. Talk about a coincidence!

Most children will color on paper that is provided for them and rarely use the walls after the initial experimentation, even if they do think it's fun to clean up. Children who repeatedly misbehave and color on walls or cupboards sometimes have other goals in mind. Subconsciously, they may be seeking revenge, attention, or power. These are three of the four goals of misbehavior that Rudolf Dreikurs identified.

The goals of misbehavior

Trying to change a child's behavior without considering the emotion or the motivating force *behind* the behavior is a bit like cutting the flower off a dandelion plant and expecting the dandelion to quit growing. We need to get to the *root* of misbehavior if we want to change it. To motivate children to change, identify the belief system that motivates their behavior.

Rudolf Dreikurs taught that there are four basic goals that motivate behavior. Typically, a child will seek to *achieve* these goals in a positive way, but when positive channels are blocked, with the result that the child is unsuccessful in meeting the goal, he will turn to misbehavior and the goals themselves will become skewed.

Goals of behavior	Goals of misbehavior
1. contact and connection	1. attention
2 personal power	2. control
3. protection	3. revenge
4. withdrawal	4. display of inadequacy

1. When the child's goal of contact is achieved and they receive healthy recognition and attention, the child is satisfied. If the child is not able to connect, he will misbehave and seek *attention* in a negative way. As we have already mentioned, children will get *attention* one way or another.

2. If the child does not feel she can exercise her own personal power, *control* will become an issue and she will seek to control others, or to "prove" that no one is going to boss her around!

3. When the child learns to assert herself and to establish healthy boundaries, she learns about fairness, and the goal of *protection* is achieved. If, however, she feels her boundaries have been crossed and she is hurt, she will desperately seek revenge, believing the best defense (protection) is a strong offense. (If your child hurts your feelings, one way to go beyond your own hurt and to get at the root of the misbehavior is to ask or think to yourself, "What could be hurting you so much that you feel you need to hurt me in order to be heard?")

4. If the child learns when it is important to surrender to the situation and to accept the things she cannot change, she achieves the goal of withdrawal and learns how to "let go." When the discouraged child feels hopeless, she gives up, believing herself to be inadequate, and avoids trying to do things. She then often looks for others to do things *for* her.

The key to identifying the goal of a child's misbehavior is to ask yourself, *"How do I feel?"* Get curious about what feelings within you are evoked by the behavior. Knowing and understanding *your own feelings* is a major clue to uncovering how to handle your child's behavior. Such awareness of your inner state is also essential to gaining control of your own inner environment. It shifts your focus from simply *reacting* to your child's behavior, trying to change it, and entering a power struggle; to assertively deciding what you will do next.

Here's an example: Your child is crying and insisting that he cannot put his shoes on himself.

On the surface, you may think that his goal is to display *inadequacy*. However, if the feeling his behavior evokes in you is irritation and annoyance (much like a fly buzzing around your head is irritating), the child's goal is more likely to be *attention*.

If you feel angry when you check in and ask yourself "How do I feel?" the child's goal is likely *power*. Perhaps the child wants to show you that you can't boss him around. It will help you to identify your feelings if you recognize the physical symptoms of anger. Is your jaw tensed, or your fists clenched? Think about where you usually feel anger first.

If you know your child can put his own shoes on and has hauled them out and made a scene in front of your friends – perhaps even throwing his shoes at you – and your feeling is embarrassment and hurt that he would do this to you, the goal of his misbehavior is likely *revenge*.

If you find yourself feeling nauseous and hopeless, almost sick inside, believing your child will never learn to put his own shoes on, his goal is likely to display *inadequacy*. He can get you to put them on for him by pretending he simply isn't capable.

Study the chart on the next page to identify your normal reaction to your child's misbehavior, your *child's* reaction to your reaction, how you can correct the misbehavior at the time, and how you can re-direct your attention in the long term so that the child does not need to act out to obtain the healthy goals of contact, power, protection, or withdrawal.

Goals of Misbehavior

Goal	How do you feel?	What do you want to do?	What is your child's reaction?	How can you correct it?	How you can redirect?
Attention	Irritated	Coax, nag, remind, beg	Temporarily stops	Ignore behavior, give attention later	Encourage & recognize involvement & contributions
Control	Angry/defeated	Fight or give in	Intensifies behavior, defiant compliance	Refuse to be drawn in, allow consequence	Recognize & encourage independence
Revenge	Hurt	Retaliate or withdraw	Seeks more revenge	Avoid acting hurt	Build trust and mutual respect; emphasize fairness
Display of Inadequacy	Hopeless	Give up	Refuses to try, is passive	Encourage all efforts; don't pity	Reassure child it's okay to be angry

Attention

In the case with the shoes, *identify how you feel,* then identify your usual response. In other words, "*What do you feel you want to do?*" If you want to *coax, nag, remind, or beg* your child to stop crying and to get his shoes on, and *the child temporarily stops* and tries to put them on, but starts to cry again shortly afterward, chances are good that the goal is indeed to get your *attention.* In order *to correct this misbehavior, ignore it, or distract him with something else, then give him your attention later.*

Ignoring attention-getting behavior can be very difficult, because the child usually intensifies the behavior. Now, instead of whimpering a little, he's whining a lot! Become a master of distraction, especially with young children. Shift their attention to something else and you have avoided giving attention to the misbehavior.

Giving attention to the misbehavior keeps it occurring, because the child has achieved his goal of getting attention. In the long term, *redirect your attention by making a conscious effort to encourage and recognize his involvement and contributions.* Remember to *take some time to be present with your child every day.*

Control

Perhaps you found yourself *responding in anger* to your child's insistence that you put his shoes on. *If his goal is control,* your natural inclination is to *fight back or just give in.* Do you say to yourself, "Oh, just forget it, it's easier to do it myself"? Perhaps you find yourself stuck in an argument with your child. He will likely intensify his resistant behavior *and* become even more defiant at your insistence that he put his shoes on. If you stay there and struggle over the issue, you are both stuck in the power struggle. Remember: *as soon as you find yourself caught in a power struggle, stop struggling. Breathe deeply, let go, and decide what you will do, not what you will make your child do. Refuse to be drawn in.* If possible, *allow the consequence* of leaving without his shoes, or pick him up calmly along with his shoes, and tell him he'll have to put them on in the car or on the bus. Realize that if he is struggling for power he is ready to take on more responsibility than he currently has. *Let him experience his own personal power in a positive manner.* Make a note to give him more power at appropriate times, thereby *recognizing and encouraging his independence.*

Revenge

When a child becomes vengeful, behavior becomes more violent – physically or emotionally. If *you feel hurt, perhaps even outraged*, believing your child is deliberately trying to hurt you by embarrassing you, your child's goal is revenge. You will likely *want to retaliate and get even, or withdraw* and sink into the floor. If you retaliate, the child then has a reason to fight back again, and will seek more revenge.

It is important to *avoid acting hurt* in situations where revenge is the goal. This may be difficult to understand, but think of it this way: If the child's goal is to hurt your feelings and you let him know he has succeeded, he goes, "Yes! Scored!" Remind yourself that *your child would only intend to hurt you if he himself was hurting deeply.* It is best not to react at all to your child's vengeful action, and to *work hard at building trust and mutual respect* in the long term. Look for ways to show your child he is lovable. *Emphasize fairness* in all that you do, because a vengeful child is simply trying to even the score.

Display of inadequacy

If you look at the child who insists he can't put his shoes on and *you feel sick, suspecting that the situation truly is hopeless* and that he will never learn to put on his shoes, the child's goal is likely withdrawal from the problem through a display of inadequacy. He is terrified of making a mistake and so chooses to get your help and attention by insisting he "can't," and that he never will be able to put his shoes on. You probably *feel like you just want to give up* and you envision yourself following him to high school to tie his soccer cleats. No matter what you do or say, your child refuses to even try. He doesn't act out; *he remains very passive,* but holds your attention because he refuses to try.

It is crucial at this time that you not give up, but rather *use every opportunity that you can to encourage his efforts* to do anything. Empathize with him, but *do not pity.* Sit down next to him and *validate his frustration* at trying new tasks. *Break the task into manageable steps.* Help him with one of the steps if you have to, but encourage him to take at least one step. Remember that encouragement is not judgmental praise, but a deliberate and specific description of what's working, regardless of how little that may be.

In the long term, *look deeply and see his strengths. Assure him that it is okay to feel frustrated and angry.* Often, the discouraged child who is displaying inadequacy does not feel safe to express his anger or frustration. Avoid arguing with the child who displays inadequacy: "You can do it!" "No I can't" "Sure you can." "No I can't." Remember that we tend to believe what we hear ourselves say, rather than what someone else tells us, so stop giving the child the opportunity to reinforce his negative beliefs.

Perhaps the most important section of all on the chart is the one called "How can I redirect?" Remember that building a healthy relationship with your child is crucial. Focus on using your own power in the relationship appropriately, and on encouraging your child to do the same. Work at regaining trust, allowing mistakes, and encouraging appropriate expression of emotions.

This approach emphasizes "the big picture or the long term." When we put our attention here, we are focusing on "what works." The skills you have been working with throughout this book will help you to be effective over the long term by building that strong, caring relationship with your child.

- If attention is the primary issue, reread chapter 6 on encouragement and remember to take time every day to be fully *present* with your child.
- If power struggles are at the heart of your issues, work intensely with the concepts outlined in chapter 3 and the circle of empowerment.
- If revenge is your child's main goal, pay special attention to chapter 5 on communication, and to the next chapter. Respect yourself and your child, clarify boundaries, and establish trust.
- If inadequacy and withdrawal are the issue, work intensively with

empathetic listening and encouragement, as discussed in chapters 4 and 6. Make your home a safe place for your child to make lots of mistakes, and model making mistakes yourself.

Passive, aggressive, & assertive behavior

The ultimate goal of discipline is to help children achieve self-discipline and to let them know that they *do* have power. Discipline is about choosing to exercise that power appropriately.

When a child says, "You can't make me!" agree with her. "Of course I can't make you. You have the power to decide for yourself." The key to teaching children assertive behavior, rather than having them adopt passive or aggressive behavior, is to help them understand that true power lies within themselves.

Three very simple questions determine whether actions spring from aggression, assertiveness, or passivity:

- When people are aggressive their concern is: *"What do I need to make other people do?"*
- When people act passively their concern is: *"What will other people make me do?"*
- Assertiveness means we need only take responsibility for our own behavior as we ask: *"What will I do?"*

Passiveness and aggressiveness tend to exist along a continuum, with one often attracting the other. The more passive one person becomes, the more aggressive the other becomes, and vice versa. Sometimes passivity becomes passive-aggressive behavior, where outwardly the person acts passively, often even cooperatively. Secretly, however, he acts destructively and aggressively. Stephen Glenn, in his videotape series *Developing Capable People*, likens passive-aggressive behavior to a puppy who, while he is licking your face, is peeing in your lap.

We can avoid and most effectively deal with passive and aggressive behaviors from a position of assertiveness. It's as if assertiveness exists at a higher level of thinking. Imagine a triangle.

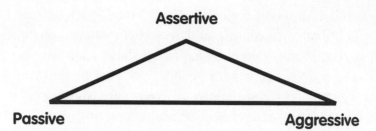

Assertive

Passive　　　　　　　　　　　　　　　　**Aggressive**

When children act passively or aggressively, lift yourself to the assertiveness perspective. Simply ask yourself, "What will *I* do?" Be very clear that it is not your job to *make your child do* anything. Focus on *your* actions, claim *your* true power, and allow your child to exercise *her* true power.

If you stay firmly rooted in respecting yourself, your child, and your boundaries, your child will eventually come to respect you, herself, and her boundaries.

Parents often become too emotionally involved when disciplining children. They become attached to controlling their child and to making her follow their rules. This is actually very aggressive behavior and it will provoke aggressive behavior in the child, or incite passivity. Only when the parent acts assertively will the child learn assertive behavior.

Teach children that they have the power to decide for themselves what they will do. However, their decision will have consequences and an effect on you, the parent. This, in turn, will affect them. They will learn to make wise decisions when they experience the outcome of their decisions. For example, you can let your child know she'll need to get herself dressed if she wants to go shopping with you. If your child does not have herself dressed and ready to go when it's time to leave, leave without her. Acting assertively means that *you* decide what *you* will do. Firmly, but kindly tell her you're sorry she won't be joining you on this shopping trip, that she'll have to walk to school or catch a bus, or that she'll have to stay home with the sitter.

With younger children, it is often more work and takes advanced planning to set some consequences into motion. You will need to arrange for an emergency sitter ahead of time, unless someone old enough and competent enough is there to deal with an upset child. This will still take less time and less energy than constantly and fruitlessly reminding your child to put her shoes on, delivering lecture 291 over and over. Just think how often we hear ourselves repeating the same lecture (perhaps the very one your parents delivered and that you swore you would never hear coming out of your mouth)! "If I've told you once, I've told you a thousand times…" so what makes us think that the thousand and first time is going to work?

Take action and stop talking and lecturing. Lecturing only destroys your relationship with your child and in the end reduces your influence and authority in their lives. You come to be viewed as "all talk and no action," or worse, "the old nag."

Your job is to remain calm as you carry out the consequence, focusing entirely on what you will do. Let your child know she will have an opportunity to join you again, and let her know when.

§

"AAAAAAAHHHHH! Don't want to goooooooooooo! AAAAAAAHHHHHH!"

My peaceful shower and time at the gym were interrupted as a young mother strode past the showers calmly carrying a screaming toddler.

"I know you don't want to go," she said between the child's screams. "I don't want to go either, but I told you we'd have to leave if you bit Mommy again."

"I'm sorry, sorry, Mommy," sobbed the distraught child, "I won't do it no more, Mommy, I promise!"

"I'm glad you won't bite again, Jodi, but we still have to go home now. I told you if you bit me again we'd have to leave. We can try again tomorrow." Mom's voice was firm but caring. Her daughter continued to scream and protest as her mother calmly dressed her, assuring her she'd have a chance to "try again tomorrow." She showed empathy for her daughter, but firmly carried out the consequences she had obviously told her daughter about earlier.

I marveled at her ability to remain calm and to focus on what she needed to do. She smiled apologetically at the women who were in the dressing room, but never wavered from her goal of dressing her child and herself and heading for home. By the time they left, her daughter had her thumb in her mouth, and was resting a tired-looking head on her mom's shoulder. "I bet she'll sleep well tonight," I thought to myself. What a marvelous example of assertiveness and discipline.

§

Your child will learn to act assertively with you as you focus on acting assertively with her. You can then help her to see the choices she has in *every* situation. Help her understand that she always has the power to decide what she will do. There is no need for her to make others do anything, and she does not need to spend her time and energy worrying about what others might make her do. Her power lies not in controlling others, but in controlling herself. When she really understands this, she will have no desire to control or bully others, nor will she allow others to bully or control her.

Managing challenging behavior

Managing challenging behavior does not depend on simply knowing *what* to do; rather, the key to effectiveness lies in *how* we approach the situation.

Treating our children with respect is essential. We are able to do this when we can look at life from their perspective.

Always keep in mind that the real purpose of corrective action is to:

- Guide your child in learning appropriate behavior.
- Help him develop a clear sense of inner direction.
- Avoid dangerous situations.
- Assert your individual rights as a parent.

Think of situations in which you might use the following techniques to manage challenging or inappropriate behavior.

- **Distract the child:** Talk to the child directly to change the topic and/or activity. For example: "Oh, look at that…" Another example of simple distraction is to say, "Oh, thank you, I've been looking for that!" At the same time, remove the item you do not want your young child to have from his hand.

- **Use indirect distraction:** Create a situation to distract your child. For example, begin playing noisily and happily with an interesting toy to entice your child away from the inappropriate behavior. *Parents of young children who become masters of distraction can avoid many potential power struggles and emotional eruptions. They may even ward off potential disasters.*

    Outside a building and at the top of a long stone stairway, a toddler escaped his mother's embrace. He ran joyfully toward the stairway. His mom realized that if she ran after him he would very likely increase his speed toward the dangerous stairs. Immediately, she called his name and started jumping up and down, doing jumping jacks. "Trevor! Look at Mom!" she called. The little guy stopped and looked, and a nearby adult, recognizing what had happened, grabbed the little boy and returned him safely to his mother.

- **Assist compliance:** Physically help a young child comply with your request. For example, lift the child off the table if she refuses to get down. Often, assisted compliance is preceded by offering choices. For example, "Do you want to walk to the car, or would you like me to carry you?"

- **Offer choices:** For example, "Do you want to eat with us now, or wait until breakfast to eat?" Both choices you offer must be acceptable to you as the parent. Offer choices in a friendly manner and then carry through with the child's decision. With older children, negotiating an agreement beforehand and following through on prearranged consequences is especially effective. For example, if the child has agreed to be in by midnight or they will forfeit the use of the car for the next two weeks, and the child arrives home later than 12:00 a.m., respectfully allow the consequence to take place. *Avoid lecturing, scolding, etc.*

- ***Ignore the behavior (not the child):*** Use this when a child misbehaves to gain attention. Sometimes the easiest way to ignore misbehavior is to remove yourself from the scene.
- ***Offer a substitute and redirect the child:*** For example, if the child is pounding on furniture with a hammer, substitute the furniture with a piece of wood, or the hammer with a soft toy.
- ***Modify the environment in one of three ways:***
  1. Add something new (such as another toy).
  2. Limit access to certain items or areas.
  3. Change environments by moving elsewhere.

     Many discipline problems can be avoided by providing children with appropriate space to run, jump, splash, pound, create, roll, tumble, read, sleep… and to just be, quietly and without pressure. Clearly defining areas where children can fulfill each of these needs can make our job as parents and caregivers easier and more enjoyable.
- ***Allow natural and logical consequences:*** Refer to previous information in this chapter.
- ***Help children to express the feelings behind inappropriate behavior:*** This is often the most effective way to dispel inappropriate behavior. When we truly listen with empathy to our child, they are able to release feelings that would otherwise erupt in negative behavior. We can accept the feelings and teach children how to drain their frustrations in an effective manner, freeing them to act in more constructive ways.
- ***Change your own attitude:*** Perhaps your expectations are not realistic. Are your standards too high? Are you assuming your child knows something she may not know? Are you expecting your child to act like a little adult? Shifting your own perceptions can reduce discipline hassles and open the door for a deeper, richer relationship with your child. Giving up the idea that you have to correct every little mistake your child makes and learning to appreciate your child for who they really are opens the door to true discipline.

A word about time outs

Time out is perhaps the most misused "disciplinary" method. Most parents and teachers use time out in a way that turns it into a punishment. As such, it no longer operates as an effective disciplinary method. Be aware that sending an already frustrated child into isolation, away from you, can result in further frustration and added problems in your relationship.

If you use time out at all, it must be understood by the child *and* the parent as a method of helping the child to calm down and to change his current state of being to a more centered, positive state. The environment the child spends time out in must be one where this goal is encouraged or fostered. Perhaps the parent needs to go *with* the child as he removes him from the scene of the disturbance, as well as help the child to release his frustrations and to calm down. Children can also be helped to determine for themselves when they are ready to rejoin an activity.

Again, time out should not be used as a punitive measure.

Summary

We want our children to view discipline as something to strive toward in their lives because it will help them to achieve what they want. Punishment used as discipline turns discipline into something children want to avoid at all costs. Punishment teaches children to avoid getting caught and can put children into danger. It provokes rebellion and resentment, or forces children into retreat.

Discipline is always solution-focused. Discipline empowers both the parent and the child, because it encourages assertive behavior, healthy respect, and it observes the boundaries of everyone. The question, "What will *I* do?" helps to keep both parent and child focused on inner power, and on respect for self and others. Discipline encourages children to make amends and teaches them that mistakes are for learning. Staying calm and solution-focused are keys to healthy and effective discipline.

Understanding the goals of misbehavior can help us to determine immediate and long-range steps to take in order to redirect children's behavior. Understanding these goals also helps us to address the root cause of the misbehavior and to put it into perspective in our relationship with our child.

Remember that the only true authority we have with our children is the authority they are willing to grant us through their desire to maintain a strong relationship with us. Taking time to bond with our children and to nourish a positive relationship is the strongest disciplinary approach we can take. This is because discipline is not just about correcting behavior in the moment; it is also a life-long process of helping our children to become confident people who are able to trust their own inner guidance and to make decisions that enable them to function effectively in any environment.

9

The Way of Parenting with Spirit

Honoring the highest good in you & your child and embracing delight

We are not human beings with spiritual moments;
we are spiritual beings with human moments.
— Deepak Chopra

All that I give is given to myself.
— A Course in Miracles

Whatever you can do or dream you can do, begin it.
Boldness has genius, power and magic in it.
— Johann Wolfgang von Goethe

Children have never been very good at listening to their elders,
but they have never failed to imitate them.
— James Baldwin

Perhaps love is the process of leading you gently back to yourself.
— Saint Exupery

Children do not need perfect parents, but they do need parents who
are following a path of self-discovery and healing and
who can recognize and repair their mistakes.
Having children provides us with a unique and wonderful opportunity
to understand ourselves better and
to heal the pain from our own childhoods.
— ALETHA SOLTER

Remembering De-Light is the name of a book I wrote for children, but it is really a story for all ages.

It is about a light that shines eternally and without fear, without even knowledge of fear; a light that decides to take on a lampshade, for it sees other lights have shades. At first that lampshade is clear and simple and the light shines beautifully through it. But as it moves about and encounters other shades, it notices that others have some very funky decorations and wouldn't it be cool to have some of those decorations, too? And so the light goes on a mission gathering toys, decals, and designs; it twists and turns trying to please all of the other shades. Predictably so, the light gets so caught up in decorating the shade and pleasing others that it forgets it is the light and starts to believe it is the shade. Life is, after all, where we put our attention!

Fear now enters the life of the lamp, for the shade can be destroyed without a moment's notice. It starts to build thick walls of defense, and then hustles to camouflage the ugly defenses, needing more and more decorations to do so. Soon it finds itself so caught up in the panic of gathering decorations and building defenses that it becomes very weary. In its exhaustion, it begins to smash into the other shades, blaming them for its loss of power. "If only" becomes a prominent phrase in its vocabulary.

Finally, not only its prized decoration is smashed, but a huge crack appears clear through the shade itself. The pain is so great that the lamp begins to cry, and his tears begin to melt the glue that holds the decorations. As they slip from his shade in the midst of his dark turmoil, he recognizes a light that offers comfort and an odd sense of familiarity.

And *then* he remembers – he *is* the light, and as soon as he remembers that *he* is the light, he recognizes the light within all of the other shades.

Embracing delight in your family is about remembering and recognizing the light within you and within every member of your family: seeing that light, speaking to that light, and hearing the voice of that light – for the light represents the eternal love that shines within each and every one of us. We were born with it. It is our inheritance. And much of life is a matter of uncovering that light once we have buried it.

The tools, examples, and exercises throughout this book have been provided to help you remember, in a very practical way, that you are the light and that your children, too, shine with their own light. We need not fix the shade, gathering more and more decorations; nor spin and turn to please others; nor hide behind massive walls of defense. So much of effective parenting and true connection with our children is about learning how to avoid creating situations where our children feel they must protect themselves, or hide themselves away and put on another face, another decal, in order to please us or someone else. It is about seeing their light by recognizing our own, and about allowing both to shine.

Once upon a time there was a magnificent light…

There is a tribe in Africa who assigns a very special song to each child. Before the baby is born, the mother and her friends go out in to the wilderness to wait to hear the song for her unborn child. When they return, they have the song. That song is sung only at very special occasions. When the child is born, enters education, makes the transition to adulthood, and marries, they sing his song. When he dies, they use the song to sing his spirit on. There is one other time the person will hear his song. If the child commits a crime or an aberrant social act, the community gathers to sing his song, to call him back to the path of his spirit.

**And that light shone with all the beauty and brilliance
of every star in the universe...**

We want to call forth the light in each and every one of our children, to remind them of their own spirit and goodness. I believe our job as parents is to help them discover their innate strength, inner guidance, and personal power.

For it knew its connection to the universal light force...

Helping children trust their inner guidance

How can we encourage our child to develop her intuition and to listen to the only voice of guidance that will be with her always – her own inner guidance?

First, communicating honestly and with integrity when talking with children is a powerful way to help them develop trust in their own perceptions and inner guidance. Avoid giving children mixed messages and be conscious of sending whole and complete "I messages," as we discussed in chapter 5. If something disturbs you deeply and your child senses that something is wrong and asks you about it, be honest. Don't tell him that nothing is wrong. You certainly don't have to give him all of the details, nor should you, but if you insist nothing is wrong, he learns to doubt his intuition. You can tell him that, indeed, you have been under some stress and strain, but that you are working on it. Thank him for his concern.

Second, let's stop insisting that we know better what our child needs than she does! How many of us have been guilty of that one? I've heard it said that a sweater is a garment a child wears when her mother is cold! "Put your sweater on, it's cold out there!" "But, Mom, I'm not cold!" "Put it on anyway!"

We believe we are protecting her from the cold, but let's stop and think about what message we are *really* sending her. Essentially, we're telling her it's more important for her to listen to us than to trust her own body's thermostat. We think it's important to protect her from herself (after all, we have more years of experience on this planet and we know when she should be cold). But possibly the other reason we do it is to protect ourselves from other people's judgments!

§

I REMEMBER TAKING my three-year-old daughter to the hockey rink to watch her brothers practice. I was always freezing in the rink so you can imagine my surprise when my daughter insisted on wearing a sundress! My initial reaction was, "Arleigh, go and change, you'll freeze in that!"

"No, I want to wear this," Arleigh replied indignantly, and then added, "I'm not cold."

I could sense the early warning signals of a power struggle, and I remembered to allow her to experience the consequences of her choices, so I eased off a little. I simply said, "Well, you may be a little cold when we get there. I'll pack your pants and a jacket just in case." I was certain that she would change her mind.

Well, she never did change her mind. We spent hours, sometimes days, in that hockey arena and she never once complained about being cold. Indeed, she didn't seem to *be* cold, and she never got sick because of it.

It wasn't easy, though, for me to sit there and allow her to run around in a sundress. My head was filled with thoughts of, "What will people think? What will people say?"

When my dad came for a visit, he spoke the thoughts I was so sure everyone was thinking: "How can you let her run around like that? Aren't you afraid she'll get sick?"

That's it, I thought; she'll get sick and everyone will think I don't care. Or everyone will think she's just a spoiled brat, getting to do whatever she likes. And, of course, both of those underlying thoughts would point to the judgment that I am not a good parent! Well, get over it Maggie, I told myself. Bottom line is, she's not cold, she's not sick, and the only reason she needs to put a sweater on is because you're worried about what others might think!

Today, I'm very glad I didn't insist. For one thing, it meant one less power struggle. And, of course, more important than anything else, Arleigh has learned to trust her own inner guidance and her own body's thermostat.

§

And the light started to twist and turn to please all the other lampshades…

What will people think? What will people say? What will people do?

Worrying about what people think can interfere in many ways with allowing children to trust their own inner guidance, as it becomes our theme song. Pretty soon we find ourselves in major power struggles with our children, insisting that they cut their hair, lower their hemline, make new friends. We withhold our approval, and too often our love, in an attempt to get our children to buckle under and follow our rules. And what is the driving force? Our deep-seated fears about how the rest of society will judge us if we don't live up to their standards.

Listen to the voice inside your head. How much time and energy do you spend worrying about what others will think, say, or do? Does it interfere with developing a healthy relationship with your child? Many parents have told me that they feel pressured by the judgments they perceive other people hold about them and their child. Strangers give them "the look" when their child cries in a public place and they will feel pressured to spank their child.

One day I overheard someone say something that has helped me to release the concern over what everyone else might think.

I used to worry a lot about what people would think of me, though in my 20s I pretended I didn't care what the world thought of me. In my 30s and 40s, I worried a great deal about what the world thought of me, but now that I'm 50, I realize the world was never thinking of me in the first place!

Why ruin my relationship with my children by trying to make sure they present the "correct" image to society, I thought, when society really doesn't care?

In your heart of hearts, what's more important: getting to know your children and creating healthy, strong relationships with them, or gaining the neighbors' approval? Focus on appreciating your children for who they are right now, rather than "shoulding" on them for not playing the role we expected them to play, or for not living up to standards we ourselves may feel miserable about not attaining.

Remember when your child was very young? Do you remember how you marveled at each new stage of growth he entered? Now he's rolling over, now he's crawling, he's said three new words today... I bet you didn't say, "Look kid, get it right! Here, let me show you how it's done!" You expected that he would make mistakes. After all, mistakes are part of the learning process.

As children grow older, however, parents often feel pressured to teach them the *right* way, *now*, leaving little room for mistakes that may embarrass the family in some way. We often become more demanding that our child learns it the first time, and we get upset if they make the same mistake twice. This is especially true with regard to social skills – we've already told them how to behave, now why don't they just do it?!

Imagine what might happen if we step out of our teaching role for a moment to simply appreciate the learning process in every stage of life. Instead of jumping to correct and redirect children's behavior so that it falls in line with our expectations, what would happen to our relationships and to our influence with our children if we gave them the space to learn, and gave ourselves the space to truly get to know our children as people?

We can be most effective as guides to our children when they *invite* us to guide them. Remember that the only true authority we have with our children is the authority they are willing to give us. That willingness will be based upon the strength of their desire to have a relationship with us. That desire diminishes if they experience failure after failure in living up to our expectations.

Take time to step back and observe who your children truly are. Set parental pride aside and resist the urge to instruct. Let curiosity open up your relationship and your influence with them.

If parental pride is getting in the way of developing a meaningful relationship with your children, put it in your back pocket. Miracles can happen when your first and foremost desire is simply to get to know yourself and your children.

§

A FRIEND OF MINE shared a rather tragic story of how her father was so busy trying to get his children to follow his rules, trying to prevent them from blemishing the image he wanted to present of himself to the rest of the community, that he used the greatest weapon he could think of to gain control: withdrawal of his love and support.

When she was growing up, her dad used the fear of expulsion from the family in an attempt to control his children. He'd share the latest gossip at the dinner table about how "so and so" was pregnant – for shame! Then he'd expound on the sin of the girl's predicament and warn his daughters that if they ever got pregnant before marriage, they needn't even *think* of coming home – ever again.

As you might have guessed, my friend *did* get pregnant. She was 19 and living across the country from her family. She carried the baby through the entire pregnancy and gave her up for adoption when she was born. She never told anyone and she never had another child.

But for years, she found herself tormented by the need to reconnect with her daughter. When my friend was finally in her 40s, she began a search for her daughter, found her, and decided it was time her father knew about it. He said he wanted to meet his granddaughter and, as it turned out, his great-granddaughter. He said he couldn't figure out why his daughter had kept this secret from him and had denied him the joy of knowing his granddaughter as she grew up!

Had he forgotten his suppertime sermons and his threats, or had he been so intent on preventing embarrassment to his family name that he considered the threats a mere disciplinary method?

§

When parents withhold their love, or even threaten to do so, as a disciplinary method, they are playing with fire. Both parties, the parent and the child, are sure to get burned. Children find themselves always needing to prove themselves to their parents, and parents never get to experience the joy of loving and appreciating their children simply for who they are. Parents feel they have to measure out their love and approval in order to teach their children how to behave. But as I've tried to show, we can discipline without ever having to withdraw our love for our children.

Children need to know that our love and support of who they are is unconditional. If they have to spend all of their time and energy trying to figure out what they must do to earn our love, they can never trust themselves just to be themselves and they lose their connection with their inner self – with the light of who they are.

"Protection!" said the lamp, "I need protection…"

Fears can block development

Our own fear can be one of the largest blocks to helping our child develop her own inner radar and guidance system. Certainly, our children are so precious to us that the thought of anything or anyone harming them terrifies us. In our desire to protect them from harm, it is easy to overreact and to keep them from developing the tools they need to deal with life situations.

Yes, horrendous things happen in this world. Recently, we all felt the horror of the parents whose child was abducted from her bedroom in the family home. But that fear will move in and destroy our life if we let it live inside our head, if we act in fear with our child, if we take extreme measures to protect our child from all harm. We can actually put our child in danger by *not* allowing her to develop the skills she will need to deal with dangerous situations. All life deals with threats to its existence. We cannot be there forever to protect our child. So if we refuse to allow her to face danger or hardship in any shape or form, what tools will she have to face danger when it comes her way?

❦

MY FOUR-YEAR-OLD daughter, her friend, and I visited the local school one morning. As we approached the main door, it swung open and there stood a smiling teacher, welcoming us in.

"Good morning, ladies!" he beamed.

"Morning," said my daughter.

"Good morning," I responded. I expected my daughter's friend would respond in kind. Instead, she simply lifted her chin and marched past the teacher. "Sara!" I said a little reproachfully, "Why didn't you say hello?"

"Oh," she replied simply, "I don't talk to strangers. I don't know him."

❦

How on earth can we give our children the tools to face life's challenges, if we don't teach them how to make friends, partners, and business associates out of strangers? Rather than making hard-and-fast rules such as don't speak to strangers, it's important to teach children to listen to their own inner guidance and to talk about various situations they need to avoid. We cannot anticipate every situation our child will encounter, but we can help her feel confident about handling those situations if she has had practice listening to her inner guidance.

§

I SHALL NEVER FORGET the story of the three boys who narrowly escaped abduction, saved by one boy's intuition and survival skills. Apparently, the boys were walking home from school when a car pulled alongside. The man in the car told the boys that their fathers had ordered him to pick them up and had insisted that they get in. While two of the boys readily complied, the third boy ran quickly to a neighborhood home, the police were called, and the boys returned safely home.

A journalist decided to investigate why the third little boy ran for help while the first two climbed in immediately. The journalist discovered that although all three boys knew never to take rides with strangers, the first two boys came from strict, authoritarian homes. Both were afraid of defying their fathers. The third little boy came from a home where he was taught to listen first to his own intuition, and had considerable power and responsibility in making decisions.

§

Children *do* need to be able to recognize real danger – we all do. However, if our mind and heart is clouded with constant fear, it's difficult to differentiate real threats from imagined ones.

FEAR has been described as an acronym for Fantasized Experiences Appearing Real. How much of your time and energy do you spend imagining the worst that could happen? How often does your mind weave horrendous tales inside your head about what might happen? And how many of these horror stories are interfering with your relationship with your children? Perhaps they are even *poisoning* your relationship with your children, and stopping all of you from truly living your lives.

Think about the last incident that provoked intense, uncomfortable emotion within you. How long did the incident last? How long did you carry it with you – mauling it over in your mind? And yes, I said mauling not mulling, for such thoughts and emotions seem to do battle within us. But only because we allow them to do so. Studies have shown that we have approximately 60,000 thoughts a day, and 90 percent of them we had yesterday. Now that has to have some impact on our lives! What's more, Jack Kornfield, in his book *A Path with Heart*, tells us that an emotion lasts only 33 seconds, unless we feed it with our thoughts and other emotions. However, many people are unaware of their thoughts and emotions and do not recognize that they have any power over them. Instead, their thoughts and emotions run their lives. (If you would like other ideas and resources on how to become more aware of your own thoughts and emotions, and on how to help your children to do the same, please see the resources on page 10 and the Emotions Chart on page 235.)

Many times, instead of dealing with a singular incident, parents imagine all of the possible consequences their child may face, "if this sort of thing continues." For example, a two-year-old bites another child, or a four-year-old refuses to share, or a 13-year-old eats lunch by himself at school, and the parent's mind reels off into all sorts of imaginings about their child being socially isolated for life. They play and replay the incident over and over in their mind, imagining the worst that could happen again and again. This is often what causes parents to overreact to the incident at hand. Instead of simply dealing with what is in front of us, we are dealing with the anxiety we have created in our mind and acting from that.

In his marvelous book *The Power of Now*, Eckhart Tolle reminds us of the importance of living in this moment. Right now.

Think about it. Right now, do you have any real problems? Rarely is there a problem *in this moment*. However, most of us do not live in this moment. Tolle describes the distance between where we are in this moment and where our mind has traveled to, either in fearful anticipation of the future or in regrets of the past, as the "anxiety gap." That anxiety gap has poisoned many a parent-child relationship. The cure is to remain fully here, right now, with your child. Give them the gift of your presence.

**Almost in a state of panic now,
the lamp began to accumulate more and more stuff...**

Children need your presence, not your presents!

Presents are a poor substitute for presence. In fact, they are not a substitute at all, for presents are nothing more than decorations on the shade, whereas presence is the light itself. In today's world, however, it is easy to believe that we can substitute one for the other. Billboards, radio, TV ads, peer pressure – all call out for yet another purchase. Surely our happiness can be bought! And so we get caught up in spending all of our time and energy doing things that allow us to buy our children the "treasures" that promise fulfillment. It is exhausting work and we become too weary and worn out to grace our children with true presence – our presence, the light of our Being.

There is no substitute for spending quality time with your child. She needs your presence in order to grow into her own light. Make time to share it, for both of your sakes.

**Trading and scheduling every second of his time,
running here, running there, doing this, doing that...**

Children need time just to be

Beware of scheduling every moment of your child's life. Children need time just to be – we all do. My definition of stress is "too much stuff in too-small a space." Sometimes our efforts to provide everything for our children – every opportunity, every skill, every electronic device and toy to keep them occupied and educated – creates tremendous stress and strain in children's lives, and actually robs them of the opportunity to develop their innate skills and abilities.

Developmentalists tell us that the emergent learning phase in a child's life is the most important. This is when the child goes into himself to discover what is there. This is often the time of imaginary playmates. Too many children are missing this very valuable phase of learning because they have no time for it; their lives are filled with television, video games, organized lessons, courses, and sports activities. Many families are stuck on a treadmill in this regard, for children become so accustomed to having something "out there" to keep them occupied that they whine and complain that they are bored when that "something" is missing. Parents can't stand the whining and rush to fill the gap.

If only we understood that this "gap" is exactly what children need to go through to get to the inside, *of them*. When your children are bored, instead of taking responsibility for their boredom and trying to "cure" it, tell them, "Great, I'm glad you're bored, because that's a sign for you to go inside and get to know yourself." Then leave them to be *with themselves*. Do not try to fix their boredom. Encourage younger children to explore their own inner world by choosing toys that expand their imagination and that require them to become creative and involved. Little animals, dolls, Duplo, and sand toys are examples. Remember that education means "to draw out." We want to draw the child out, rather than stuff more things in.

We all need time just to be with ourselves, "to hear ourselves think." It is during this time that we can reflect on our life from a higher level of consciousness and start *to create* rather than *react*. Try taking one hour per day to spend just with yourself. Spending that time in nature can be especially powerful. The key is not to turn on the TV or radio, or to pick up the phone or newspaper or your favorite book. Spend time with just you – your thoughts, your feelings, and your spirit.

And the light started to stumble about, blaming all the other shades; believing that somehow they had robbed him of his power…

Blaming hurts the blamer most

Outside stimuli and extrinsic motivation have become such a large part of our society that we tend to look outward for everything: for someone to solve our problems, for someone or something to make us happy; for someone else to take responsibility and to do our work for us. And so it follows that when things don't go our way, we also tend to blame others.

Blame strips us of all of our power. If we protest that "it's not my fault, so I can't do anything about it," we have put ourselves in the victim role. When we insist that someone else makes us mad, we have given them the power to fix our problem with our anger. Now how likely are they to come rushing in and do that? They are probably happy to have that kind of power over us.

Often, one parent will blame the other when things are not going well with their children – or at least when things are not going the way they want them to go!

Sometimes we make unspoken agreements with our partners or our children: "I will make you happy," we say. How many of us have been raised to make someone else happy? I grew up believing that it was my job to find a man and make him happy. Then and only then would I find my own fulfillment. Well, I found a man who wanted me to make him happy and I tried very hard to do so. The problem was that there were many times when he was *not* happy, and guess who was to blame? I tried harder, but to no avail. The only thing that happened was that we both became miserable. You see, the fundamental flaw in our agreement was that neither of us fully understood that *it is not possible to make someone else happy*. We are all responsible for our own happiness. We can feel happy when we are with others, but they do not *make* us happy. Happiness is a state of being. We must all find it inside ourselves.

When we take responsibility for other people's emotions, we rob them of the opportunity to grow and to learn to take responsibility for themselves and for their own lives. This makes parenting an especially difficult job; after all, we are responsible for our children's health and welfare for a good portion of their lives. It is never our responsibility, however, to fix their boredom, their depression, or their unhappiness – which doesn't mean that we aren't concerned, or that we don't take extra time to be with them, to listen to them, or to look for help if necessary. Sometimes we focus as much as we can on what we can do, yet we still see the situation with our child crumbling.

֍

TYLER HAD ACADEMIC problems at school from day one, it seemed. He had tremendous difficulty reading and copying things from the board. We had his eyes tested and he was prescribed glasses, which helped a bit. However, the problems with reading and writing continued. By November of grade 3, Tyler was reading at a grade 1.5 reading level.

I knew Tyler was a bright boy, but neither his teachers nor I were able to help him. That is when I went looking for help and that is when I met Beverly Hunter, a woman I have come to know and admire for the incredible work she has done helping many children work through learning disabilities. When Bev tested Tyler, she realized right away that he could not track more than three or four letters at a time with his eyes. No wonder he was having difficulty reading and copying from the board – he was copying letter by letter rather than reading the words and phrases. Bev also discovered that Tyler could not do a cross-crawl; that is, touch his right elbow to his left knee, alternate elbows and knees and keep going. She physically manipulated his limbs to show him the movements. (The cross-crawl and eye tracking are skills babies learn when they crawl. Tyler never crawled but stood up at nine months old and ran!)

Before we saw Bev, I had noticed that Tyler looked a little strange skating. After meeting with Bev, Tyler's skating changed as soon as he got onto the ice (the cross crawl is the skater's movement). That winter, he practiced the cross-crawl at least three times a week, every time he played hockey. In April, he was retested and read at a 3.7 grade point reading level. Today, he is an honors student and sometimes makes the principal's list.

֍

Sometimes we *do* need help to bring out the strengths and abilities our children possess. The focus must always be on bringing out *their* strengths to deal with the situation, however. I did not take responsibility for Tyler's happiness, nor for his school marks. I did, however, recognize that he needed help I could not give him in developing his strengths.

No one can hurt us without our consent

Teach your child that no one can hurt him unless he allows them to.

§

MY DAUGHTER'S ECZEMA made her a target of ridicule when she was young. The girls in her room would run away from her saying, "Eczema girl is here, run!" I spent hours and days and weeks and years empathizing with her, but not seeing her as a victim. We talked a lot about true power being within her, about not allowing the girls to have such power over her that it changed her idea of who she was. We talked about how others must be hurting and fearful to strike out to hurt someone else. She found great comfort in recognizing that everyone has challenges or "flaws" to overcome; it's just that hers were more obvious because of her eczema.

Together, we wrote a story about a tree that had to struggle all its life to get enough moisture. It stood in the strong wind and harsh weather. It faced lightning and snow storms, and it grew into a beautiful and interesting shape because of its trials and tribulations. Not far away from this tree, however, grew a cultured, well-manicured tree. It was watered every day and sheltered from most storms. It grew straight and tall and was quite beautiful, but not really interesting to look at. Then one day a giant cyclone hit their area. The tree in the wilderness dug deeply into the ground with its roots. The cultured tree tried to hold on with its roots as well, but its root system was very shallow, for it had never had to struggle to survive, or to send its roots down deep to look for moisture. As you can imagine, only the wilderness tree survived.

That story helped my daughter to see that her experience with eczema could help her to find her own strength. Today I admire her strength and courage, and her firm grasp of power and response-ability.

§

Every problem brings its gift

Do not be too hasty to jump in and solve all of your children's problems. I believe that no problem comes our way without a gift attached to it. Problems call up our inner strength, a strength that is just waiting to be used.

§

PARENT-TEACHER INTERVIEWS had never been Joan's favorite meetings to attend and this one had her more leery than any of the others. Joan noticed the slight limp as Jordon's teacher greeted them.

"Come on in – have a seat. I'm just going to stand. My back's been bothering me lately," he said, offering a weak smile.

No wonder Jordon calls him grouchy, thought Joan. He must be in constant pain. Her mind wandered back to the day Jordan had decided to tackle his problems with this teacher head on…

"Oh man, I hate that dorky teacher of mine!" Joan's nine-year-old son burst through the door in a fit of rage. *Oh-oh,* thought Joan, *what's happened now?* She didn't have long to wait as her son tromped up the stairs and into the kitchen. "You know what he did *today,* Mom?"

"No, what?"

"He made Devon, Jud, and me wait behind the rest of the class goin' to assembly, and then we had to stand with him at the door to the gym while everybody, *everybody in the whole school,* stared at us as they filed by. And then if that wasn't enough, he led us by the hand to our seats! Oh man, I *hate* him!"

"Wow, that must have been embarrassing," Joan empathized with her son.

"No kidding! Why does he have to pick on us? He's always pickin' on us!"

"Well, what was happening right before that?" Joan asked, truly curious.

"Nothing, he just hates us." Jordon sounded a little defensive.

Joan didn't want to put Jordon on the defensive. Her goal was to help him express his feelings around this. "You feel like he just does these things to make you miserable."

"Yeah, he never does that to anyone else, and it's not like we were foolin' around any more than anyone else – we weren't even really foolin' around. Devon just made a joke and we were laughing. It's like that all the time; other people can do stuff and he doesn't say anything. But even if I don't agree with him he'll come right up to me and lower his glasses so he looks me right in the eye and say, 'Isn't that right, Jordan?'"

"Like he's trying to intimidate you." Joan was trying hard to put herself in her son's shoes.

"Yeah, but I don't let him. I just look straight back at him and say, 'No, Mr. Karrin, I don't think it is.' Mom, can't you see if I can move to another class?"

Joan had already considered this strategy. This was not the first time Jordon had come home so upset. But suddenly, a light went on inside her head. Her reply to Jordon's request surprised her as much as it surprised her son. "You know what, Jordon? This guy is going to be one of the best teachers you've ever had."

"Mom, what's the *matter* with you – aren't you *listening*?!"

"Yes, Jordon, I am – and it sounds to me like you already know how to handle Mr. Karrin. You don't let him intimidate you even when you think that's what he's trying to do – and it sounds like you handle the situation respectfully, with equal respect for yourself and your teacher. You don't lip him back, but you stand your ground and don't let him push you around."

"Yeah, so…?" Jordon was a little puzzled.

"Jordon, this is your chance to use your gift. You've always had a very special gift of relating to everyone, regardless of his or her age or position. Here's your chance to develop it and make it powerful in your life."

"What d'ya mean?"

"You can run away from this situation or you can use it to your advantage. See it as a test of your strength – your ability to remain respectful, but to still stand up for yourself and your friends."

"Oh! I get it," the lights went on in Jordan's eyes. "So today I could have asked him to explain specifically what we did that everyone else wasn't doing."

"Yes!"

"And I could'a told him I didn't think it was fair."

"You got it."

"Tomorrow I'm gonna talk to him."

"Go for it."

And Jordan had gone for it. Today, they'd hear the teacher's perspective…

"Jordon's marks are about average," the teacher was saying, "but one thing I've noticed is that he handles himself very well."

"Thank you, Mr. Karrin," said Jordon. Then, much to

everyone's amazement, he continued on: "Now about these lines…"

"What about them?" asked his surprised teacher.

"Well, I don't see the point of them," Jordon stated bluntly.

"If you do something wrong, Jordon, then you have to write lines," came his teacher's simple response.

"But I don't see how that makes anything right," Jordon protested.

"Well, what do you think should happen, Jordon?" His teacher sounded a little impatient.

"If I do something wrong, then maybe I can do something to make it right," Jordon replied with perfect calm.

Mr. Karrin looked really perplexed now as he asked, "Well, like what?"

"Well, if I was running in the halls, maybe I should have to hang out until everyone has left and help you patrol the halls."

"But Jordon, that takes longer than writing the lines! Most kids would rather just write the lines and be gone."

Jordon and Mr. Karrin never did reach an agreement on that one. Mr. Karrin seemed determined to hang on to his line-writing punishment no matter what.

As for Joan, she was positively glowing with the pride she felt in her son. *Surely this is the best education he's had,* she thought. *How many skills are more valuable than the ones he's displayed here tonight?*

Joan heard a number of stories of how Jordon learned to handle himself that year. One of the most powerful came toward the end of the year…

According to Jordon, Mr. Karrin was screaming at some kids at the front of the class. (Apparently, Jordon wasn't the only one the teacher picked on!)

"I wonder who peed in his cereal?" Jordon whispered to his friend.

"Jordon! What was that?" Mr. Karrin demanded sharply.

"I was just wondering what was bothering you, Mr. Karrin, because I don't think those kids like to be yelled at like that," Jordon replied quietly.

This must have caught the teacher completely unaware, and much to his credit and to everyone's surprise, he seemed to shift gears and asked the rest of the class, "Oh, was I yelling?"

Their heads bobbed affirmatively in unison.

"Oh, I didn't meant to," he mumbled apologetically. "It's just that I've been in so much pain lately with my back."

When Joan heard this story, she smiled inwardly. Yes indeed, she thought, there was a very good reason Jordon needed to remain in Mr. Karrin's class this year. Perhaps Jordon *and* his teacher had learned a lot, one from the other.

§

It is so important to lift ourselves above the trenches of habit and reaction that may not be in the best interest of our children or ourselves. Lift yourself to a level where you can see life in its entirety. Ask yourself, "What is the lesson I'm to learn in this situation?" In his book *Illusions*, author Richard Bach says, "A cloud does not know why it moves in such a direction at such a time, but the sky knows, and if you lift yourself above the clouds you, too, will know why your life moves in the direction it does." Seeing and living from a higher perspective is essential in dealing with challenging situations. Even the act of *looking* for the lesson is helpful, because it takes us out of the trenches.

A friend of mine was counseling a young mom whose son had been diagnosed with ADHD (Attention Deficit Hyperactivity Disorder). The mom was at the end of her rope when my friend told her that this situation would not be in her life if she did not have the strength and the ability to deal with it. "Such situations are in our life to help us to develop our innate gifts," she said. My friend added that she believed the child had chosen this young mom to be his parent. Suddenly the young mom's face relaxed as she began to view her situation from a higher perspective. She stopped struggling against the situation and accepted it fully. (So often it is our struggle against what *is* that makes our life so difficult.) The young mom resolved to discover her innate gifts and abilities that would allow her to deal with this situation and to give her son the guidance he needed. She began to see her son's behavior as a chance for her to develop the strength and patience necessary to deal with his spontaneous and often outrageous behavior.

> **Here in the midst of his dark turmoil,**
> **was a light – a light that offered comfort and**
> **an odd sense of familiarity…**

Unconditional love

Perhaps this child had come into her life to teach her strength, patience, and the power of acceptance of this moment. Even though she had not felt like she had received unconditional love from her parents, she now began to experience unconditional love as she extended it to her son. She experienced joy in simply giving. For when one gives unconditional love, giving and receiving become one. In the moment of truly giving, we receive, for the joy is in the giving. If we give and then wait to receive, we will always be disappointed. We will be weighing the weight of our gift with the returning parcel and we shall always feel guilty or cheated – guilty because our giving is not enough, or cheated because the return is too little.

I am not talking about the kind of giving that occurs when parents say, "I give and give and give and get nothing in return."

"All that I give is given to myself." Holding this phrase from *A Course in Miracles* in my mind has helped me to understand how to give unconditionally. It has also helped me to realize that to be loved I must give love, and that love is a feeling, a *power* that is generated from within.

Very young children are wonderful teachers of how to love unconditionally. When they give us a big beautiful smile, they give it entirely because it feels good for them to do so, and they give it without any expectation or need for return. They simply shine from who they are. They *are* the light. *If we allow them to,* they take us into the *now,* this moment, for there is no other moment for them; they are fully immersed in the present and in presence. Of course, they are not always smiling in that presence, but once their emotional upset is passed, they do not carry grudges from the past, nor spend their time fearing the future. They simply are, and they accept us as we are, readily forgiving and forgetting anything we may have done. They don't judge things as good and bad. They simply see things as they are and deal with the situation right now, as it is. It is only as they mature that they begin to worry about the past and the future, and to judge people and things as good or bad. Perhaps they learn to do so from us.

Giving unconditional love does not mean that we don't discipline our children. Not at all. Discipline is a loving way to help our children gain the skills, habits, and abilities that will allow them to create a life worth living. Giving unconditional love does not mean that we don't tell our children how we feel when we are upset or angry. They need to learn how to function in relationships and we are their main teachers in this. They therefore need to hear how their actions have affected others. When we tell them how we feel, we speak honestly, sincerely, and respectfully. We speak without blame and we speak to their strength to resolve the issue.

Partners in parenting

"Yes, but how do I get my partner on board with me?" It is difficult enough, in this job of parenting, to align our actions with our values, but what about those of our partner?

Many marital struggles arise because we see our partner's actions as being out of alignment with our own values. And this is in relation to the most important and precious people in the world! "How is my partner's behavior affecting my child?" we ask ourselves. "What if I don't think that what s/he's doing is what's best for my child? What if it damages him? How can I get my spouse to change, become more involved, less critical, less wishy-washy, less this and more of that?"

This is the theme song that destroys many marriages and nearly all partners sing it occasionally. We get trapped in the game of wanting to change our partner while ferociously defending our own position.

> **And the shade that once provided a healthy boundary**
> **now became a major barrier –**
> **a blockade to his life's energy…**

If this is what you are battling with, rather than insist that your partner read the book and use the skills with your children, it is likely to be more powerful and effective if you use all of the skills we've discussed to not only bring out the light in your children, but to bring out the light in your spouse as well. Invite your partner to discuss and explore important values and dreams you have for your family and yourself. Creating a Family Vision Statement (see chapter 2) is a very powerful way to help both of you dig deeply into your values and to decide what is truly most important to you. Generally, I have found that when people explore their deepest values and the concerns that they have for their children, they find that their core values are very similar; it is just that people tend to weight values differently.

Perhaps your partner is not willing or ready to do that exercise yet, and is very resistant to reading books or watching videos on this subject. Some people have found that inviting their partner to discuss the quotes that begin each chapter is a powerful communication tool. If you choose to do this, remember to "seek first to understand" your partner's point of view before honestly expressing your own. Stay in the moment and do not allow yourself to refer to or to respond to any blameful statement of past incidents.

The highest in me salutes the highest in you

Namaste is an East Indian greeting meaning, "the highest in me salutes the highest in you." It is also a philosophy I remind myself to apply to my parenting. Of course, sometimes I slip up and hear myself saying, "Listen up here. I'm the parent and you're the child and I expect you to listen to me!" (Sometimes I have to ask myself, "Who am I trying to convince?") The trick is to catch myself in those states, to let go, to shift to experiencing the highest in me, and to seek to address the highest in my children. That does not always happen as instantaneously as I would like it to. Sometimes I have to leave the scene, calm down, get my emotions under control, and then return to speak with my children. I have found that, in my family, we all respond to this approach and function much more happily and efficiently when I use it, for when I approach my children from this perspective they naturally gravitate toward it.

"Indigo children" is a term being used to describe a new group of children being born today. Some people describe them as an evolutionary advancement in the human race. Super-sensitive, very intuitive, highly intelligent, and often extremely active, these children are sometimes misdiagnosed with ADHD (Attention Deficit Hyperactivity Disorder) or ADD (Attention Deficit Disorder). They do not buy into the traditional systems of parenting and schooling in our society. They insist on mutual respect in every relationship they have and refuse to acknowledge adults as superior simply because they have lived more years. Many adults find this very difficult to deal with and choose to tighten constraints and punishments in an attempt to force these children into compliance, because that has been the traditional way of raising children. (There was a period in our history not too many decades ago when "breaking the child's spirit" was an accomplishment many parents boasted of.) These children are forcing the adults in their lives to deal with them at the elevated level of consciousness we have been talking about here.

Deepak Chopra reminds us that, *"We are not human beings with spiritual moments, but spiritual beings with human moments."*

How would your life change if you lived as a "spiritual being with human moments rather than as a human being with spiritual moments?" What a powerful paradigm shift that creates! Indigo children insist that we address them from this level of thinking and being. Then, they will be able to develop and use their gifts to enhance society, and will help us all to live with greater personal power, freedom, and insight. If you suspect you have an Indigo child, paying special attention to the issue of personal power, respecting healthy boundaries, and solution-focused discipline will be most effective in relating to her.

Indigo children are not the only children who benefit from this philosophy of parenting, however. How could one possibly go wrong if one seeks to parent from the highest and deepest understanding of their own worth and value, addressing the highest worth in their child?

> "We are not human beings with spiritual moments, but spiritual beings with human moments."
>
> – Deepak Chopra

When we dig into our deepest values, explore them, confirm them, and live them, we bring our values into alignment with our actions. I call this "core integrity," and much of the stress of living occurs when we live outside of it. We know we hold these values, but somehow they've been buried in pressures and demands from the outside world, and our actions are not aligned or integrated with them. That is stress.

I find it critical to take time to explore who I am and to allow myself to flow from the inside out; to allow myself, *in this moment*, to experience myself as the light and to glow.

> **As he recognized his own light,**
> **he began to look at all of the other lamps.**
> **Suddenly, not only could he see through his shade,**
> **he could see through theirs, too,**
> **clear through to their light...**

Role reversal

Sometimes it's essential to step back from the roles, rules, and obligations we have lived by for so long in order to get to know who *we* are underneath it all. Only then will we really get to know our children, for only then do we release them from the expectations we have about their roles, rules, and obligations.

Think about the roles and rules you live by. Are they helping you in your relationship or hindering you? I'm not suggesting you relinquish all of them. Some we must uphold. We have a responsibility to care for our children and when they are young that responsibility can be all-consuming. This is when it is most important to make time for ourselves and to remember who we are in our essence, before we were Mom or Dad. It is so important to do what keeps us joyful, and sometimes that means challenging the traditional roles that have been set out for us.

§

REVITALIZED AND INVIGORATED after my long walk in the hills, I burst into the house. The enticing aroma of freshly baked cake greeted my nostrils and like a character in the cartoons, I followed the wafting scent right up the stairs and into the kitchen. I was starving! A piece of cake was just what I needed – or so said my salivating taste buds anyway.

I found my 14-year-old son just removing a marvelous chocolate cake from the oven.

"Oh, that smells good, Tyler!" I bent my head directly over the cake and inhaled deeply. "Ahhhhhhhhh…" I patted the top with my finger and it sprang back immediately. "Perfect," I said. "Tyler, you're such a wonderful baker."

Tyler smiled wanly and I continued, "So, Tyler, can we have some now? Can we?" The thought of sinking my teeth into a piece of cake was so exciting that I found myself doing a little jig right then and there.

Tyler turned to face me, an oven mitt still on one hand and the other hand on his hip. "Mom," he said sternly, "don't you think there's something *wrong* with this picture? I mean, isn't it supposed to be the other way around? Aren't I supposed to be the one dancing around begging for cake and *you* the one baking it?"

There was a split second of silence as we each captured a comic snapshot of this scene in our mind, and then we both burst into laughter. I gave Tyler a big hug and a peck on the cheek and replied simply, "Not if we really expect to eat cake!"

§

Honoring what brings me joy and keeps me connected to my light makes it so much easier to recognize the inner glow in my children, and in all life forms. It's very helpful to keep some of my attention in any given moment focused on the light within me.

Living your life

Parenting is a tough job. Our children begin life totally dependent upon us. Gradually, we must step back in order to allow them more and more independence, until finally we let go completely and send them off into the world.

Letting go requires practice; again and again we are asked to let go with our children. They can dress themselves now, walk to school by themselves, stay out until midnight, drive a car… That letting go is so much easier if we stay centered in our own light and keep building our own dream. Carl Jung says, "Nothing has more psychological impact on the lives of children than the unlived lives of their parents."

I shared that quote with a young friend of mine who was in grade 12. I could tell it hit home with him from the look in his eyes. "Whoa," he said after a long pause. "Is that ever the truth. You know, I'm so confused about what I'm going to do next year. My parents really want me to take science and math and become a doctor, but that's their dream, not mine. I love the arts – music, fine art, drama – but they tell me I'll never make a living. There's a lot of pressure to become a doctor. There's a lot of pressure to live their dream, because they didn't live it themselves."

Your children are watching you. You can best inspire them to live their dreams by living yours. You inspire them to be all that they can be

> "Nothing has more psychological impact on the lives of children than the unlived lives of their parents."
>
> – Carl Jung

by being all that *you* can be. Making time for yourself and taking care of you and your dreams is not selfish; it is essential to the happiness of your family; it is essential to the health of your children. You will not "find" this time to look after you; you have to take it; you have to create it. It takes great strength, energy, and courage to live one's life from one's passion and values, but at least when you get to the end of your life, you will have truly lived.

Summary

Your presence is required in your relationship with your children. Reach deeply within yourself and connect from the depth of who you are to the depth within your children. Be all that you are, and you will encourage your children to be all that they are. Teach them to know and to trust their own light and inner wisdom.

Let go of the fears that block development and that keep you in a state of resistance. Surrender to the moment and accept what is. Stop twisting and turning to please the world and live from your own highest vision of what is important to you.

Love your children and yourself unconditionally, with deep appreciation and reverence for the life within. Know that every challenge you or they encounter in life carries with it a gift, an opportunity to discover and strengthen your awareness of your own light and inner qualities.

Let your light shine, and know that as you do so your children will feel free to shine their own light in this world. As we reclaim our light and our personal power, the world becomes a brighter place. There is no need to drag people kicking and screaming out of the darkness and into the light. We need only let our light shine as a welcome invitation to others to do the same. This is a revolution from within, and together we leave the darkness behind.

EMOTIONS

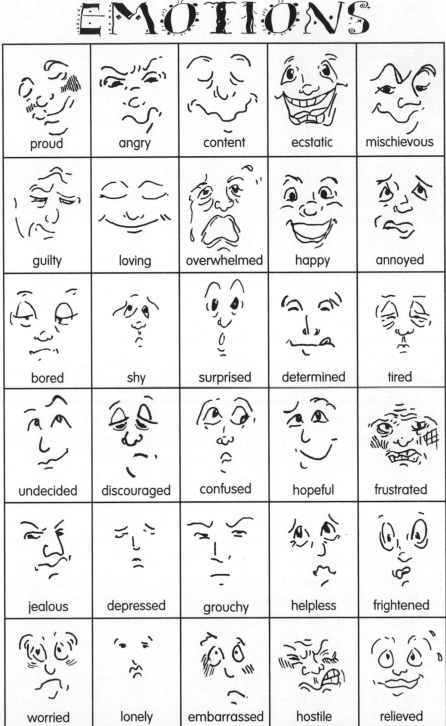

proud	angry	content	ecstatic	mischievous
guilty	loving	overwhelmed	happy	annoyed
bored	shy	surprised	determined	tired
undecided	discouraged	confused	hopeful	frustrated
jealous	depressed	grouchy	helpless	frightened
worried	lonely	embarrassed	hostile	relieved

Index

A

B

C

D